INVESTMENTS

A Self-Teaching Guide

JOEL G. SIEGEL, Ph.D., CPA
Queens College
City University of New York

JAE K. SHIM, Ph.D.
California State University at Long Beach

A Wiley Press Book

JOHN WILEY & SONS, INC.
New York • Chichester • Brisbane • Toronto • Singapore

Acknowledgments

We wish to thank our wives, Roberta Siegel and Chung Shim, for typing the manuscript. Roberta also assisted in the preparation of the figures and illustrations. We express our gratitude to Elizabeth G. Perry for her outstanding and significant editorial contribution. Donna Ryan served as the developmental editor and did an excellent job with writing style. Laurie Sleeper, Katherine Schowalter, and David Sobel are to be commended for their valuable assistance in the production stage. We received excellent comments regarding content from our eminently capable reviewers Mark Heller and Gerald Krefetz.

Publisher: Stephen Kippur
Editor: Elizabeth Perry
Managing Editor: Katherine Schowalter
Design, Composition & Make-Up: G&H/SOHO, Ltd.

Library of Congress Cataloging-in-Publication Data

Siegel, Joel G.
   Investments : a self-teaching guide.

   "Selected investment publications"—p.
   1. Investments. I. Shim, Jae K. II. Title.
HG4521.S56   1986   332.6'78   85-26422
ISBN 0-471-82351-1

Printed in the United States of America
86 87 10 9 8 7 6 5 4 3 2 1

PREFACE

Investments: A Self-Teaching Guide provides a thorough explanation of the investment selection process. The presentation is logically built up step by step so the reader can learn "how to do" investment analysis. The book is filled with self-study questions, examples, and problems to ensure that the investor has mastered the key concepts, applications, and strategies. Illustrations are given of the analytical points made. Self-tests are also provided at the conclusion of each chapter.

We hope this guide will be of value to undergraduate and graduate students taking an investments course. It can be used to supplement a standard text. Much financial, accounting, and tax information has been included. It is also designed for those seeking professional certifications such as that for Chartered Financial Analyst. Individuals working in security selection or recommendation should find it helpful, too. Included here are security analyses employed by brokerage firms, mutual funds, banks, insurance companies, and other institutional investors. And finally, we hope this book will aid those who are simply interested in learning about investments.

The guide covers investor objectives, types of investments, security markets, security transactions, sources of investment information, microcomputer applications to financial analysis, appraisal of risk and return, fundamental analysis, technical analysis, equity and debt securities, stock options, future contracts, gold, real assets, portfolio analysis and management, and investment strategies.

JOEL G. SIEGEL
JAE K. SHIM

HOW TO USE THIS BOOK

The purpose of *Investments: A Self-Teaching Guide* is to give you a strong, general overview of the basic concepts and techniques of investing. It is called a Self-Teaching Guide because you should be able to learn the subject matter with little or no difficulty if you follow the instructions. This guide has been designed to allow you to skip portions of the text that you already understand and to pinpoint concepts that you need to review.

Each chapter opens with a list of objectives for you to master. If you feel you are already familiar with these particular investment points and are knowledgeable enough to skip all or part of the chapter, turn to the end of the chapter in question and take the Self-Test. The results will tell you which sections of the chapter to study. If you answer all questions correctly, you are ready to begin the next chapter. If the material is new to you, or if you choose not to take the Self-Test, read the chapter in its entirety.

At the end of each chapter is a Review consisting of questions and answers that highlight the topics covered in the chapter and test your understanding of them. If you find you are having trouble with certain parts of the Review, go back to the appropriate sections within the chapter and reread them. When you feel ready, take the Self-Test that follows each Review section to be sure you have mastered the chapter's content. After you take the test, compare your answers with the answers given. If you miss questions about a specific topic, go over that topic once more.

By the time you complete this book, you should have a strong understanding of the investment process and all that it involves.

CONTENTS

INTRODUCTION 1

Objectives

When you complete this chapter, you will be able to:

- Consider the differing objectives of the investor in selecting an appropriate investment
- Apply taxes in the investment process
- Define risk
- Understand the risk-return trade-off
- Define an investment
- Provide the reasons for investing
- Give examples of types of investments
- Discuss short-term and long-term securities
- Understand the positive and negative aspects of each investment vehicle

Getting Started as an Investor

Before you invest any funds, you should evaluate your present financial condition. Consider your income, expenses, taxes, future prospects for higher earnings, and all other details that affect your monetary situation. Decide how much you want to invest. Then very carefully formulate your investment aim or aims. Will you invest in order to earn a profit? As a hedge against economic fluctuations? To build up a retirement income?

Your next step should be to examine the investment choices presented in this book and then decide which kinds of investments are best for you.

Set your long-term goals first, thinking in terms of the middle and distant future. Then establish short-term financial objectives that are consistent with the longer-term aims. After six months or a year, if you haven't been able to meet your short-term goals, you may have to reevaluate the long-term objectives. If, however, you have done much better than you expected to do, you may want to formulate more ambitious goals.

In the beginning, look for liquid investments that provide a good return (high interest or dividends) and are at the same time immediately salable. That's what liquid means—that you can sell the investment quickly in case you need the money for another, more important purpose. Here are some popular liquid investments:

- Certificates of deposit
- U.S. Treasury bills (T-bills)
- Money market certificates
- Mutual funds
- Savings accounts
- Commercial paper

We'll discuss other marketable, or liquid, investments later on.

Liquidity is not your only consideration, of course. You must also take into account the return you will receive on an investment—especially in relation to the risk it involves. *The higher the risk, the higher the return should be*; this is an unfailing rule of the investor.

Income on investments comes in one of three forms:

- *Ordinary income*: interest or dividends
- *Short-term capital gain*: the profit you earn when you sell an investment you've held for six months or less
- *Long-term capital gain*: the profit you earn when you sell an investment you've held for longer than six months

Taxes

Your tax situation will affect your investment choices. Many people in the lower income-tax brackets choose to invest for the purpose of increasing ordinary income, which is fully taxable (except for the first $100 in dividends received). Those in higher tax brackets, however, often choose long-term investments because they carry certain tax advantages.

Let's take a quick look at the way some securities are taxed:

- Ordinary income (interest and dividends) is fully taxable.
- Short-term capital gain is fully taxable.
- Long-term capital gain gives you a tax advantage in that only 40% of this gain is taxable.
- Income on U.S. government securities is subject to federal income tax but exempt from state and city taxes.
- Income from municipal securities (issued by your state or city) is exempt from both federal and local taxes.
- Individual retirement accounts (IRAs) and Keogh Plans provide taxable in-

come when payments are received after retirement. Prior to retirement, interest income earned on the accounts is accumulated in the fund and is nontaxable.

Now let's look more closely at some of these investments. Municipal securities, for example, look good in the list above because of the tax benefit. There is a slight catch, however. These investments usually have a long *maturity period*; in other words, you have to tie up your money for several years before you receive your profit. They are nevertheless attractive to some investors, depending on their tax bracket. An investor in the 40% bracket, for example, may hold municipal securities that provide a 10% return; this person will receive a before-tax return of 16.7% calculated as follows:

$$\frac{10\%}{1 - \text{tax rate}} = \frac{10\%}{1 - .4} = \frac{10\%}{.6} = 16.7\%$$

Tax-exempt municipals, tax deferred investments, and tax shelters such as real estate are attractive to high-tax-bracket investors.

Retired people generally favor safe investments that provide fixed yearly returns. Appreciation in the price of a security is not as important to them as a stable, guaranteed income. For example, a long-term government bond will satisfy most retirees' needs. Risky investments are not desirable because of the uncertainty.

You have to plan for sufficient income during your retirement. In addition to Social Security and your job's pension plan, you can invest in annuities and self-sponsored retirement plans like IRAs and Keoghs. You can deposit as much as $2,000 a year in an individual retirement account (IRA), the income from which is nontaxable. If you are self-employed, or if you earn significant income from self-employment in addition to your salaried job, you can deposit up to 25% of that part of your income in a Keogh Plan—also nontaxable. However, payments you receive from the fund after retirement are taxable.

Loss

We spoke earlier about capital gain and the conditions under which it is taxable. Now let's discuss capital loss. This loss is the negative difference between the price you pay for an investment and the price you receive for it when you sell it. In other words, if you buy ten shares of a certain stock for a total of $500 and later sell those shares for $350, you take a capital loss of $150.

Capital loss can be short term or long term. If you hold your $500 worth of stocks for less than six months before you sell them, you take a short-term capital loss. If you own them for more than six months, you suffer a long-term capital loss. Here's how capital losses affect your taxes:

- You must calculate your net gains and losses for both short-term and long-term investments before you do your taxes.
- You can deduct net short-term capital losses in full up to $3,000. If your losses exceed $3,000, you can carry the excess forward to the succeeding years.

- You can deduct only 50% of your long-term capital losses up to $3,000. Excess losses can be carried over to successive years with their 50% deductible.

As you can see, your best move is to sell stock before the six months are up if that stock is losing money.

Risk

How much financial risk should you be willing to take on an investment?

Risk is the chance you take of losing money on an investment; it is the uncertainty regarding the investment's final payoff, in other words. The more an investment can vary in value during the maturity period, the greater the risk you take when you buy and hold on to it. Most investors favor safe investments over risky ones.

All investments involve some degree of risk. In general, you will have to find a balance between risk and return: the higher the risk, the greater must be the return. We will discuss this subject further in Chapter 3.

Types of Investments

The two basic types of investments are (1) *financial assets* and (2) *real assets*.

Financial assets comprise all intangible investments—things you cannot touch or wear or walk on. They represent your equity ownership of a company, or they provide evidence that someone owes you a debt, or they show your right to buy or sell your ownership interest at a later date. Financial assets include the following:

- Common stock
- Options and warrants
- Mutual funds
- Savings accounts and money market certificates
- Treasury bills
- Money market funds
- Commercial paper
- Bonds
- Preferred stock
- Commodity futures
- Financial futures

Real assets are those investments you can put your hands on. They are what we call real property.

Real assets include the following:

- Real estate
- Precious metals
- Gems
- Collectibles
- Common metals
- Oil

In other words, any land that you own is a real asset. If you collect antiques, artworks, rare books, or vintage cars, your collection constitutes a real asset. The most commonly collected precious metals are gold and silver; investors in precious gems may collect diamonds, rubies, or emeralds. Copper, oil, natural gas, and other exhaustible resources also constitute real assets.

Real assets are investments you can hold on to all your life or sell for a profit when they have appreciated to your satisfaction.

In this book we will be concerned largely with financial assets.

Direct and Indirect Investments

When you make a direct investment, you acquire a claim on a specific property. When you choose an indirect investment, you invest in a portfolio of securities or properties. One popular indirect investment is a share of a mutual fund, which is a portfolio of securities issued by any one of several mutual fund investment companies.

The typical investor has a portfolio (collection) of securities representing diversified investment types. This variety of investments minimizes risk while bringing in a satisfactory return.

Long-Term and Short-Term Investments

An investment may be short-term or long-term. Short-term investments are held for one year or less, whereas long-term investments mature after more than one year. An example of a short-term investment is a one-year certificate of deposit (CD); a typical long-term investment is a ten-year bond. Some long-term investments have no maturity date—equity securities (common stocks and preferred stocks), for example. However, you can buy a long-term investment and treat it as a short-term investment by selling it within one year. How many of your investments are short-term? How many are long-term? Is that the combination you consider best for you?

Short-term securities involve little risk and offer liquidity. They include the liquid investments listed earlier in this chapter: savings accounts, certificates of deposit, money market certificates, mutual funds, U.S. Treasury bills, and commercial paper.

Long-term securities are debt instruments with a maturity of more than one year. (A *debt instrument* is a certificate or security showing that you loaned funds to a company or to a government in return for future interest and repayment of principal.) Equity securities are also long-term investments. Let's look at long-term investments one at a time.

Bonds are one type of debt instrument—a certificate of corporate or government obligation to you in return for your loan (investment). Bonds are usually sold in $1,000 denominations. You can purchase or sell a bond before maturity at a price other than face value. The *bond indenture* specifies the terms of the borrowing arrangement. Many bonds are callable at the command of the issuing company. This means that the issuing firm can buy back the debt prior to maturity.

The interest you receive on a bond equals the nominal interest rate times the face value. Suppose, for example, that you buy a ten-year $40,000 bond at

8% interest. You pay 94% of face value. Interest is payable semiannually, which is typical. The purchase price is $37,600 (94% × $40,000). You receive a semi-annual interest payment of $1,600 (4% × $40,000). At maturity, you will receive the full maturity value of $40,000.

Look for quotes (current prices) of bonds in such newspapers as the *Wall Street Journal.* You'll find financial data related to specific bond issues in *Moody's Manual* and the *Standard and Poor's Bond Guide.*

Corporate bonds are riskier than government bonds because companies can fail. Most individuals in high tax brackets do not find corporate bonds attractive because interest received is fully taxable.

U.S. government obligations include Treasury notes and Treasury bonds. Treasury notes are U.S. obligations having a maturity from one to seven years. The yield is slightly higher than on treasury bills. Treasury bonds are long-term obligations up to 35 years. They usually pay a higher interest rate than do Treasury notes. The risk of default is nonexistent.

The interest on local (state and city) bonds, as we said earlier, is exempt from federal and local taxes. However, to be free from state tax you must buy bonds issued by your home state. For example, interest on New York State bonds is exempt from New York State tax, but interest on California bonds is not exempt from New York tax. Municipal bonds appeal to high-tax-bracket investors because the interest received is tax free. If you are in a high tax bracket, you should consider buying municipal bonds.

Zero-coupon bonds have no coupon rate, so there is no interest payment. The bonds are issued at a discount and redeemed at face value at maturity. Tax-exempt investors may be interested in these bonds because only the annual increase in price is taxable.

The interest rate on *variable rate bonds* is changed to keep the bonds at par. Investors desiring stability in principal may be attracted to these bonds.

An *equity* investment is ownership in a business (evidenced by a security) or property (evidenced by title). You obtain an equity interest by buying stock. Equity securities have no maturity date. You purchase them in order to receive income (dividends) and capital gain. Two types of stock are common and preferred. Different classes of stock (A;B) may also exist.

Common stock is an equity investment reflecting ownership in a company. If you hold 1,000 shares of common stock in a firm that has 1,500 shares outstanding, you own a 66.7% ownership interest in that company. Thus, you can control the company. In many instances an investor can gain control by owning a considerably smaller percentage than this.

Here are some of the advantages of owning common stock:

- You earn the right to vote in company elections.
- If the company does well, your stock price will appreciate and your dividends will increase.
- Common stock is a better hedge against inflation than are fixed-income obligations.

Owning common stock also carries disadvantages, however. These disadvantages include the following:

- When the firm isn't thriving, your earnings will drop and price stability will suffer—meaning that the stocks' resale value will decrease.
- You may not receive sizable dividends.
- Common stock is riskier than debt securities and preferred stock, since you will be the last to receive money if the company fails. (Debt holders come before equity holders in liquidation, and in this instance you are an equity holder.)

Common stock owners have the *preemptive right*, which allows them to maintain their proportionate share in the company. Thus, they can buy new shares issued before they go on sale to the general public. This way they can maintain their percentage of ownership.

Preferred stock holders have no voting rights but they do receive a fixed dividend rate. They also take precedence over common stock holders in the receipt of dividends and in the event of liquidation. Preferred stock may be callable at the company's option, and it generally provides only dividend income, with no capital gain potential. See Table 1.1 for a comparison of debt instruments, preferred stock, and common stock.

Table 1.1 **Comparison of Securities**

	Debt	Preferred Stock	Common Stock
Voting rights	No	No	Yes
Risk	Lowest	Medium	Highest
Appreciation in value of company	No	Yes	Yes
Fixed annual return	Yes	Yes	No
Partial tax exclusion for interest or dividends	No	Yes($100)	Yes($100)

There are various types of stocks:

- *Blue chips* stocks in the strongest and largest companies—IBM, for example.
- *Growth stocks* in companies like certain high-tech firms show a faster rate of growth than those of other businesses. They usually pay low dividends and have low yields because they retain funds for growth.
- *Income stocks* provide above-average returns.
- *Cyclical stocks* vary in price depending on changes in the economy.

The two types of dividends are cash and stock. *Cash dividends* are taxable, except for the first $100 as previously noted. They are usually paid quarterly. If a stock dividend differs from the security receiving the dividend (in other words, if you own common stock but get a preferred stock dividend), you must pay taxes on the dividends you receive. If they are the same (in other words, if you own common stock and get common stock dividends), you do not pay taxes on those dividends. You can look up the dividend records and ratings of companies in *Standard and Poor's Stock Guide*. Companies with good dividend histories are listed in Table 1.2.

Table 1.2 **Corporations with Good Dividend Yields**

Exxon Corp.
Maytag Co.
Mobil Corp.
Pacific Lighting
Standard Oil (Cal.)
Texas Utilities
Xerox Corp.

Convertible securities can be converted into common stock at a later date. Two examples of these securities are convertible bonds and convertible preferred stock. These securities give you fixed income in the form of interest (convertible bonds) or dividends (convertible preferred stocks). They also let you benefit from the appreciation value of the common stock.

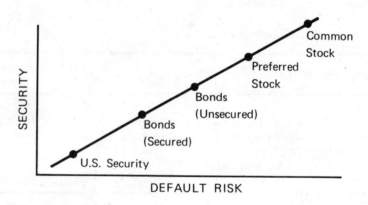

Figure 1.1 *Risk Chart*

Rights, Options, and Warrants

Fractional share rights give you the privilege of purchasing a fraction of one share of common stock at a set price for a specified period of time. For example, you might have a fractional share right to acquire one-fifth of a share of common stock at $40 per share, or you might have 400 rights and thus have an opportunity to obtain 80 shares (1/5 × 400) at $40 per share. Rights typically have a life of no more than three months. The value of a right lies in the chance to purchase stock at less than its market price.

An *option* is the right to buy security or property at a given price during a specified time period. An option is neither a debt nor equity; it is an opportunity to acquire securities. You might buy options in order to take advantage of an anticipated change in the price of common stocks. You should know, however, that you, as an option holder, have no guaranteed return; the option may not be attractive to exercise, because the market price of the underlying common stock has not increased, for example, or the option time period may elapse. If this happens, you will lose your investment. Hence, options involve considerable risk.

A *warrant* allows you to buy a given number of shares at a predetermined price during a specified time period. Each warrant allows you to acquire one or more shares of stock. At time of issue, the price (e.g., $60 a share) exceeds the market price (e.g., $55 a share), but warrants generally have a life of several years. Thus, if the market price goes up (e.g., $70 a share), your warrant allows you to buy the stock at $60 per share, which is now *below* the $70 market price.

Other Forms of Investments

Commodity and *financial futures* are seller commitments to deliver a specific commodity or financial instrument at a set price by a given date. The profitability of these investments depends on many uncontrollable factors linked to the world economy. Therefore, futures are high-risk investments.

Real estate—investments in land and buildings—is a good investment during inflation. However, a very large capital investment is usually required.

Gold and silver are a volatile investment, but they do provide a hedge against inflation. The price of precious metals tends to increase during troubled times and decrease during stable, predictable periods. When interest rates are high, it is expensive to invest in gold or silver. You can buy different forms of gold or silver for investment purposes:

- Bullion—gold or silver bars or wafers
- Coins
- Gold or silver stocks—shares in a company that owns gold or silver mines
- Gold or silver futures contracts

Precious gems such as diamonds and rubies appeal to investors because of their small size, ease of concealment, and durability. They are most popular in countries whose paper currency is unstable.

Collectibles include art, stamps, and antiques. They offer profit potential as well as aesthetic enjoyment. If you plan to invest in collectibles, you must thoroughly understand current market conditions and the variables that influence your collectible's value. Information about collectibles sometimes appears in *Money, Collector/Investor,* and *Antique Monthly.*

Table 1.3 **Returns and Inflation**

What Does Best During Inflation?
Real Estate
Common Stock
What Does Poorly During Inflation?
Fixed Income Securities

Review

1. **(T,F)** The only objective of investing is to make a return.

   False. Return maximization ignores the problems of time and risk. The goal of investing should be to maximize the present value of the investor's ownership. This is accomplished by maximizing the return rate and minimizing risk. Thus, the investment process must take into account return, risk, and time.

2. All of the following are short-term investments *except*
   a. Treasury bills
   b. CDs
   c. bonds
   d. money market funds

   c

3. The dividend tax exclusion is $_____.

   $100

4. What types of investments might be best for those in high tax brackets?

   municipal bonds which are not taxable; real estate and other investments that provide tax credits or tax shelters

5. Define and discuss the tax treatment of a long-term capital gain.

   A long-term capital gain is the sale of a security held more than six months where the selling price exceeds the initial cost. Of this gain 40% is subject to tax.

6. An investor is in the 40% tax bracket. He receives 6% interest on a municipal bond priced at $100. The taxable equivalent yield is:
   a. 8%
   b. 12%
   c. 10%
   d. 9%

   c

7. An investor buys a bond for $900. Six months later she sells it for $1,000. The interest rate on the bond is 8%. The tax rate is 25%, (a) What is the after-tax return on the bond? (b) What would the answer be if the bond were a municipal bond?

a. Interest   8% × $1,000 $80
    After-tax rate (1 − .25)   ×.75
    After-tax interest $60
    Long-term capital gain $1,000 − $900 $100
    Long-term capital gain deduction   ×.40
    Subject to tax $40
    After-tax rate   ×.75
    After-tax capital gain   +30
    Total after-tax rate of return $90
    After-tax rate of return as a percent of purchase price:
    $90/$900 = 10%

b. Interest on a municipal bond is not taxed, but capital gains are.
    Interest $80
    Capital gain   +30
    Total after-tax rate of return $110
    After-tax rate of return as a percent of purchase price:
    $110/$900 = 12.2%

8. Retired investors generally favor _____ securities.

    fixed income

9. You must strive for an acceptable balance, or trade-off, between _____ and _____.

    risk, return

10. (T,F) A government security has absolutely no risk.

    False. It is possible for a government security to default.

11. _____ investments reflect either equity or debt ownership.

    Security

12. Property investments are either _____ or _____.

    real, personal

13. What are the two basic types of investments?

_____

financial assets and real assets

14. Compare direct and indirect investments.

_____

A direct investment involves the acquisition of a direct claim to a security or property like a share owned in General Motors. An indirect investment is an indirect claim to a security or property like a share owned in a mutual fund that has a portfolio of securities.

15. (T,F) Treasury bills are not good investments for idle cash.

_____

False. Treasury bills are good outlets for excess temporary cash since they are marketable and safe, with an assured return.

16. Why might one want to invest in a mutual fund?

_____

professional management; diversification for small investors

17. What is commercial paper?

_____

It is unsecured notes issued by large businesses of the highest quality. They require a minimum investment of $25,000, and they mature in 30, 60, or 90 days, or up to six months. The return on commercial paper is greater than the return on U.S. Treasury bills.

18. List several long-term investments.

_____

stocks, bonds, real estate, and gold

19. The interest paid on the face of a bond is referred to as _____ interest.

_____

nominal (coupon)

20. Corporate bonds are in $_____ denominations.

_____

$1,000

21. (T,F) A call provision is of benefit to bondholders.

_____

False. Although the issuing company usually has to pay a premium to call in its bonds, the bondholders do not benefit in the long run. Bonds are usually called when interest rates are low, so the bond-holders have to reinvest their money at lower rates.

22. **(T,F)** Municipal bonds are fully exempt from federal tax.

False. Interest income is tax-exempt on municipal bonds, but capital gains on the sale of the securities are taxable.

23. Which type of security is most severely affected by changing interest rates?
    a. Treasury bill
    b. common stock
    c. preferred stock
    d. long-term bond

    d

24. How does the expectation of a decline in interest rates affect the price of a bond?

    The bond price increases.

25. When is the yield on a bond greater than the nominal (coupon) rate?

    The yield on a bond exceeds the coupon rate when the price falls below its par value.

26. _____ give the investor fixed interest and also appreciation value in the common stock.

    Convertible bonds

27. _____ bonds do not have interest payments.

    Zero-coupon

28. **(T,F)** Common stock is a fixed income security.

    False

29. The dividend rate on preferred stock is _____.

    fixed

30. **(T,F)** Preferred stock holders have no full voting rights.

True. Preferred stocks are ownership shares, but they do not bestow full voting rights on their owners. However, preferred stock holders may be given some voting privileges if dividends are in arrears. Full voting rights belong to common stock holders.

31. What are the differences between blue chip stocks, growth stocks, income stocks, and cyclical stocks?

Blue chip stocks are common stocks in large, financially sound, stable, mature companies. They are high-quality stocks with a long-standing record of dividends and earnings. Growth stocks are shares in companies that have a fast growth in sales, earnings, and market share. Income stocks pay higher earnings than average returns. Cyclical stocks are shares in companies whose profits vacillate with the business cycle and are compounded by it.

32. Attractive stocks that pay good dividend yields are referred to as
   a. speculative stocks
   b. developing stocks
   c. income stocks
   d. blue chip stocks

---

c

33. A company whose earnings grow faster than the U.S. economy and industry in general is referred to as
   a. a growth stock
   b. a cyclical stock
   c. a defensive stock
   d. a high flyer

---

a

34. Dividends are usually paid _____.
   a. quarterly
   b. annually
   c. monthly
   d. semi-annually

---

a

35. **(T,F)** Warrants have a longer life than options.

_____

True

36. **(T,F)** Commodity contracts are low-risk investments.

_____

False

37. **(T,F)** Gold prices typically rise in difficult times and fall during stable periods.

_____

True

38. **(T,F)** Precious metals are a hedge against inflation.

_____

True

Self-Test

1. Your tax rate is 45%. How much tax must you pay on a long-term capital gain?
2. What is the maximum tax deductibility of net short-term losses?
3. Mrs. T's marginal tax rate is 30%. What is the fully taxable yield comparable to a 6% tax-exempt yield?
4. The optimum way to avoid market risk is to
   a. purchase speculative securities
   b. invest in high-quality preferred stock and bonds
   c. invest in inflationproof securities
   d. extend the maturity date of holdings
5. Collectibles are _____ assets.
6. Short-term investments have a maturity of _____ or less.
7. _____ is an unsecured promissory note having a maturity of six months or less and issued by the highest quality companies.
8. What is a bond indenture?
9. **(T,F)** Interest on municipal bonds is tax free, but capital gains are not.
10. A bond without interest payment is referred to as a _____.
11. A $50,000 bond with a coupon rate of 14% is purchased at 102. Interest is payable semiannually. What is
    a. the purchase price of the bond?
    b. the semiannual interest payment?
    c. maturity (face) value?
12. What is a preemptive right?

13. A stock having a good dividend yield is a
    a. speculative stock
    b. growth stock
    c. blue chip stock
    d. income stock
14. The lowest-risk stock is called _____.
15. (T,F) If a preferred stock holder receives a stock dividend in common stock, the dividend is free.
16. (T,F) Commodity contracts have significant risk.
17. In troubled times, the price of _____ increases.

Self-Test Answers

1. 45% × 40% = 18%
2. $3,000
3. $$\frac{6\%}{1 - .3} = 8.6\%$$
4. b
5. real
6. one year
7. Commercial paper
8. A bond indenture contains the terms and conditions of the bond agreement.
9. True
10. zero-coupon bond
11. a. $51,000
    b. $3,500
    c. $50,000
12. The preemptive right permits current stockholders to keep their proportionate ownership share in the company. Stockholders can subscribe to new shares based in proportion to their ownership percentage in the old capital structure.
13. d
14. blue chip
15. False
16. True
17. gold or silver

INVESTMENT PROCESS AND INFORMATION

2

Objectives

When you complete this chapter, you will be able to:

- Describe the various types of securities markets
- List the functions of organized exchanges and the over-the-counter market
- Explain the role of the investment banker
- Cite the functions of the stockbroker
- Discuss the various security transactions
- Enumerate the participants in the investment process
- · List the steps in the investment process
- Explain the types of brokerage accounts
- Name various market averages and indexes
- List the sources of economic data
- Mention sources of information about the investment industry
- Name available electronic databases

Securities Markets

Suppliers and buyers of funds make their investment transactions in either the *money market* or the *capital market*. In the money market, short-term debt securities with a life of one year or less are bought and sold. Transactions in long-term securities like stocks and bonds are made in the capital market, which is composed of several security exchanges.

Capital markets are either primary or secondary. In the *primary market*, new shares are issued to the public. A new security issuance usually involves an investment banking firm that specializes in selling new security issuances for compensation. In large issues, the investment bankers act as stockbrokers that sell a percentage of the issue. The lead investment banker is the *originating house*, and all other investment bankers are the *syndicate*.

The *secondary market* is where securities are traded after their original issuance, when the original holders sell their shares to other buyers. The secondary markets include the organized security exchanges—New York, American, and regional—and the over-the-counter market. These organized exchanges serve as clearinghouses for those who supply securities and those who demand them. The listing requirements for companies on the New York Stock Exchange are more restrictive than those for the other exchanges. Table 2.1 shows companies on the New York Stock Exchange that have performed well over the years.

Table 2.1   **Companies with Good Performance Over the Years**

AT&T
Delta Airlines
Emerson Electric
General Electric
International Business Machines

"Listed" securities are traded on the organized exchanges. Trading is done on the floor of the exchange by members who are for the most part brokerage firms. Brokers bring together the buyer and seller of a stock. The New York Stock Exchange accounts for about 80% of the total volume of shares traded on organized exchanges. Regional exchanges include the Pacific Stock Exchange, which is an auction market, and the Philadelphia Stock Exchange.

The over-the-counter market is not a specific institution but a way of trading securities. Although it is not an auction market, it does provide a forum where new unlisted issues are sold. Traders (dealers) use a telecommunications network called the National Association of Security Dealers Automated Quotation System (NASDAQ) for transactions in these securities. The over-the-counter market trades a higher dollar volume of securities than do the national and regional exchanges.

Each over-the-counter trader makes a market in certain securities by offering to buy or sell them at specified prices. Dealers are the second party to a transaction. The *bid price* is the maximum price the dealer offers for a security. The *ask price* is the lowest price for which the dealer will sell the security. The dealer's profit is the *spread*—the difference between the bid price and the ask price.

What are the advantages of purchasing stocks in the over-the-counter market?

- Some securities are traded only in this market.
- Some securities have significant potential for return but with high risk.
- Over-the-counter dealers have the excellent communications network known as NASDAQ, which results in a high degree of marketability for their stocks and a better reflection of true price.

The disadvantage of buying on the over-the-counter market is that the companies whose stocks are sold there are generally lower-quality firms than those listed on the New York Stock Exchange and the American Stock Exchange.

Some listed New York Stock Exchange securities are traded on the over-the-counter market. These transactions constitute the *third market*. The *fourth market* comprises the trading of securities between institutions without the use of middlemen. Especially large issues are traded on this fourth market.

Future contracts for future delivery of a commodity or financial instrument at a given price for a specified time period are traded on several exchanges, principally the Chicago Board of Trade. This exchange has the most comprehensive listing of commodities and financial future contracts. Other future exchanges exist, some of which specialize in particular commodities. Futures in foreign currency are primarily traded on the International Monetary Market, which is part of the Chicago Mercantile Exchange.

Security Transactions

You invest when you use your own money to purchase real assets (like property) or financial assets (like securities). You make an investment to earn interest or dividend income and also perhaps because you hope your investment will increase in value so that you can later sell it at a price considerably higher than the price you paid for it. The return on your investment will depend on the type of security transaction you choose, the maturity term of the investment, and the inherent risk. In general, the longer the maturity period, the greater the return must be to compensate for the prolonged uncertainty.

Investors of funds and recipients of funds usually come together by way of a financial institution or a financial market. In some cases, however, buyers and sellers of property may deal directly. For example, financial institutions like savings and loan associations take deposits from investors and then use the funds for loans or investing. Financial markets are places where investors and suppliers of funds are brought together through intermediaries. Financial markets include stock markets, bond markets, and options.

Before you invest, you should learn the procedures for acquiring an investment, the associated costs, the characteristics of your chosen investment, and the advantages and disadvantages of alternative investment opportunities.

Stockbrokers can buy and sell securities for you. They also provide price quotations and other investment information, and they will give you stock and bond guides that explain and summarize the activity of securities.

Stockbrokers work for the brokerage houses that own seats on the organized exchanges. Members of the exchange execute orders placed by their brokers. Orders for over-the-counter securities are carried out by dealers who specialize in certain securities. Regardless of which market your security is being sold in, you have to place your order with a broker. He or she will send you a monthly statement listing the stocks you have bought and sold, the commission fees you've paid your broker, the interest charges, your dividend and interest income, and your final balance.

The brokerage firm usually holds on to stock certificates, keeping them under a "street name," so that the broker can sell them without having to get your signature.

Some of the major brokerage firms are Merrill Lynch Pierce Fenner and Smith, Shearson Lehman/American Express, Paine Webber, E.F. Hutton, Salomon Brothers, Dean Witter Reynolds, and Prudential-Bache.

Here are the different types of brokerage accounts from which you can choose:

1. *Single or Joint.* Are you single or married?
2. *Cash.* You must make full payment for securities purchased within five business days. When you sell your securities, the brokerage house has five days to give you your money.
3. *Margin.* You make partial payment for securities purchased, with the remainder on credit. The broker retains the securities as collateral.
4. *Discretionary.* You give your broker permission to buy and sell securities at his or her discretion.

Types of securities transactions include:

1. *Long purchase.* You buy a security expecting it to increase in value (buy low and sell high). Your return will come in the form of dividend and interest income over the maturity period plus capital gain at the time of sale minus brokerage fees.
2. *Short selling.* Here you will sell high and buy low. In a short sale, you'll earn a profit if market price of the security declines. To make a short sale the broker borrows the security from someone else and then sells it for you to another. Later on, you buy the shares back. If you buy the shares back at a lower price than the broker sold them for, you will make a profit. You "sell short against the box" when you sell short shares you actually own (not borrowed shares). You lose money when the repurchase price is higher than the original selling price.

   Suppose that you sell short 50 shares of stock having a market price of $25 per share. The broker borrows the shares from you and sells them to someone else for $1,250. The brokerage house holds on to the proceeds of the short sale. Later on, you buy the stock back at $20 a share, earning a per share profit of $5, or a total of $250.
3. *Buying on margin.* A margin purchase is made partly on credit. Margin requirements are generally about 50% cash and 50% credit. Typically, you have to put up more cash for equity securities than for bonds because of the greater risk. You must pay interest to the brokerage house on the money you owe them. When you buy on margin, you can make a high return or incur a significant loss, so be careful.

   Let's say that you buy 50 shares of Texas Instrument stock at $40 per share, or $2,000. The margin requirement is 60%, so you pay $1,200. The $800 balance represents a loan from the brokerage house. If the interest rate is 12%, you'll pay an annual interest charge of $96 (12% × $800). The brokerage fee is $50. Buying on margin can result in a greater return because you make only a partial payment for stock that has appreciated in value. If the stock goes to $45 one year later, you can sell it for $2,250 ($45 × 50 shares). Your profit before interest and brokerage is $250 on an investment of only $1,200. The return rate is 20.8%.

4. *Odd lots* and *round lots*. An odd-lot transaction is a transaction involving fewer than 100 shares of a security. A round-lot transaction involves units of 100 shares each. If you buy 50 shares of Company XYZ, for example, you make an odd-lot purchase. If you buy 235 shares of Company DEF, you make a combination round-lot and odd-lot transaction.

5. *Block trade*. A block trade is an order for a minimum of 10,000 shares.

You can place several kinds of orders with your broker:

1. *Market order.* You transact a market order when you purchase or sell stock at the current market price.

2. *Limit order.* This means buying at no more than a given price or selling at no less than a stated price. Your broker continues the order until a specified date or until you terminate it. Let's say that you place a limit order to buy at $10 or less a stock now selling at $11. If the stock goes up to $20, your broker will not buy it; if it falls to $10, the broker buys it immediately.

3. *Stop-loss order.* This is an order to purchase or sell a stock when it rises to or drops below a given price. Suppose that you own 1,000 shares of Avis, having a current market price of $50 per share. You give your broker a stop-loss order to sell this stock if it slips down to $46. By selling the shares at a predetermined price, you are protected from further stock price declines.

4. *Time order.* This order tells your broker to sell at a specified price during a given time period or until you cancel the order. Maybe you want to sell 50 shares of Emerson at $40 per share, and you believe the price of the stock will rise to $40 in two weeks. You place a time order with your broker to sell your Emerson shares at $40, specifying a limit of two weeks.

When you buy and sell securities, you'll have to pay transaction costs. In general, the brokerage fee on a stock transaction is between 1.5% and 3% of the transaction value. When you sell, you'll also have to pay state transfer taxes and a small federal registration fee. Can you avoid these costs? Yes, if you do not need full brokerage services, you can use a discount broker. These brokers' fees range from 30% to 70% of the fees charged by full-service brokers. You can also negotiate commissions with your broker.

Investments involve different degrees of risk. Which is riskier, government securities or gold? Obviously, gold. High-risk investments like gold are referred to as *speculative* investments. Speculation is purchasing an investment whose future value and expected return are unpredictable. It is basically short-term trading with the hope of obtaining a higher profit in the form of capital gain but with greater risk. A speculator is not interested in dividend or interest income. Do you have any speculative investments? If so, is the return you are getting adequate for the high risk?

Investment Information

What information do you need before making an investment? Depending on the investment, you should be aware of economic conditions, political environment, market status, industry surroundings, and company performance. Investment information is either descriptive or analytical. *Descriptive* information tells you about the prior behavior of the economy, politics, the market and the particular investment. *Analytical* information consists of current data including forecasts and recommendations as to specific securities. Both kinds of investment information help you assess the risk and return of a particular choice and enable you to see whether the investment conforms to your objectives.

Can you get "almost free" investment information? Yes, from newspapers and magazines. You'll have to pay for additional information from a financial advisory service publication like *Value Line*. Your local library may have these publications. The many other sources of investment information include market data and indexes, economic and current events, and industry and company data.

Market Information and Indexes

Market price information provides past, current, and expected prices of securities. Data on current and recent price behavior of stocks are contained in *price quotations*. You can get quotations directly from your broker or from a *ticker*—an automated quotation device with a screen on which stock transactions on the exchange floor are immediately reported.

Price quotations also appear in newspapers and electronic databases. IBM, for example, is listed in the *Wall Street Journal* as 123. That is the price you will pay to buy one share. Table 2.2 shows a typical price quotation.

Table 2.2   **Stock Price Quotation**

| 12-Month | | | | Yld | P/E | Sales | | | | Net |
High	Low	Stock	Div	%	Ratio	100s	High	Low	Close	Chg.
360	180	XYZ Co.	6	2.0	25	13	360	350	350	−2

Stock market indexes show how the market is doing and assist you in picking the right stocks at the proper time. The behavior of the market is important: if the market is down, a particular company—even though it is financially sound—may not do well.

Stock market averages are the mathematical average prices of a group of stocks for a specified time period. These indexes measure the present price behavior of a group of stocks relative to a base value established at an earlier time. To evaluate the strength of the market you must compare the averages and indexes at various times. A *bull* market exists when prices are rising. A *bear* market exists when prices are falling. Bear markets since 1960 are reported in Table 2.3.

Table 2.3 **Bear Markets Since 1960**

Year
1977–1982
1973–1974
1971
1968–1970
1966
1961–1962
1960

Source: Adapted from Ben Branch, *Fundamentals of Investing* (Santa Barbara, Calif.: Wiley, 1976), p. 160.

The *Dow Jones Industrial Average* (DJIA) is an average of the performance ratings of 30 industrial stocks having wide ownership and volume activity as well as significant market value. Dow Jones calculates separate averages for public utilities, transportation, and the composite. It is a composite average made up of thirty industrials, twenty transportations, and fifteen public utilities. The DJIA, which shows market trends, is the most commonly referred to stock market average. Here is a list of the companies included in the DJIA:

Allied Corp.
Aluminum Co.
American Can
American Tel. & Tel.
Bethlehem Steel
Dupont, E.I.
Eastman Kodak
Exxon Corporation
General Electric
General Motors
Goodyear Tire
Inco, Ltd.
International Business Machines
International Harvester
International Paper

McDonald's
Manville Corp.
Merck & Co.
Minnesota Mining & Mfg.
Owens-Illinois
Philip Morris
Procter & Gamble
Sears, Roebuck
Standard Oil (Calif.)
Texaco, Inc.
Union Carbide
U.S. Steel
United Technologies
Westinghouse Electric
F.W. Woolworth

Standard and Poor's has five common stock indexes. The S & P Index compares the present price of a group of stocks to the base prices from 1941 to 1943. The S & P indexes are industrial (400 companies), financial (40 companies), transportation (20 companies), public utility (40 companies), and composite

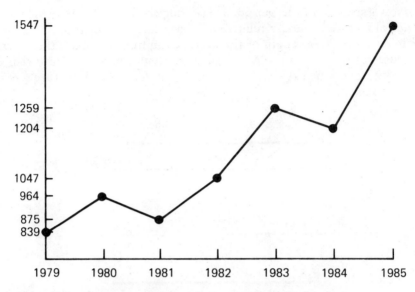

Figure 2.1 *Dow Jones Industrial Average: Year End Index*

(500 companies). S & P also has indexes for consumer and capital good companies as well as low-grade and high-grade common stocks.

The *New York Stock Exchange Index* includes all the stocks on the exchange. The *American Stock Exchange Index* reflects the price changes of its stocks. The *National Association of Security Dealers Automated Quotation (NASDAQ) Index* shows activity in the over-the-counter market. Its composite index consists of approximately 2,300 companies traded on the NASDAQ system.

Barron's puts out a 50-stock average as well as the average price of the 20 most active and 20 lowest price stocks. Other averages and indexes are published by *Moody's* and *Value Line. Value Line* includes a composite of 1,700 companies as an illustration of the overall behavior of the stock market or particular segments of it.

Indicators of bond performance also exist. Bond prices are stated as a percent of par. Bond yields show the return the bondholder receives if he or she holds the bond to maturity. Bond yield is discussed in detail in Chapter 8. In general, the yield on a bond includes annual interest income and capital appreciation. Bond yields are generally quoted for a group of bonds of similar type and quality. You'll find bond yield information in various sources including the *Federal Reserve, Standard and Poor's, Moody's,* and *Barron's.*

Economic and Current Events

By studying and analyzing economic and current events, you can learn to predict national and international economic trends. You should make a habit of reading the *Wall Street Journal* or *Barron's*, the financial section of a good general newspaper, and such business magazines as *Forbes, Fortune, Business Week, Dun's Review,* and *Financial World.*

To learn how the national economy is doing, you might also read the *Federal Reserve Bulletin*. It includes a summary of business conditions; statistics on employment, retail prices, and other relevant trends; and the Federal Reserve Board Index of industrial production. It also gives information about gross national product and national income as well as interest rates and yields.

Every month the U.S. Department of Commerce issues the *Survey of Current Business* and *Business Conditions Digest*. The *Survey* includes a monthly update by industry of business information about exports, inventories, personal consumption, and labor market statistics. *Business Conditions Digest* publishes cyclical indicators of economic activity including leading, coincident, and lagging.

Subscription services provide data regarding economic and corporate developments. They also publish forecasts of business trends and detailed economic data and analysis. One such service is the *Kiplinger Washington Letter*.

Industry and Company Analysis

Investment analysts—or security analysts, as they are sometimes called—furnish recommendations to clients for a fee. Some also manage their clients' investment portfolios and give tax advice.

Investment advisers include stockbrokers, trust department bank officers (who invest funds held in trust for clients), employees of subscription services, and investment advisory firms. Most advisory firms employ specialists in certain industries or types of portfolios.

Investment analysts usually select an industry that looks good before they pick a particular company. You can get industry data yourself from trade publications on a particular industry such as *Public Utilities Fortnightly*.

Financial services provide financial information and analysis, but most of them do not make recommendations. Examples are *Standard and Poor's*, *Moody's*, and *Value Line*. Financial advisory reports usually present one company's financial history, current financial position, and future expectations. Up-to-date supplements are issued. Examples of the materials published by some services follow:

1. Standard and Poor's publishes *Corporate Records, Stock Guide, Bond Guide, Dividend Record, Industry Survey*, and *Opportunities in Convertible Bonds*.
2. Moody's publishes manuals, *Bond Record, Bond Survey*, and *Stock Survey*.
3. Dun and Bradstreet issues *Key Business Ratios* and *Billion Dollar Directory*.

Brokerage reports analyze companies and make recommendations to buy, hold, or sell certain stocks. They also offer investment strategies and analyze specific industries and companies.

You can find corporate financial data in a company's annual report in the form of financial statements and disclosures. This will be discussed in Chapter

4. Securities and Exchange Commission (SEC) Form 10-K contains detailed information on companies that have securities listed on the stock exchanges.

Microcomputers and Electronic Databases

A microcomputer can give you immediate access to business data. It will also enable you to analyze that data quickly and to compute a rating for all of your funds or stocks. Programs are available for recordkeeping, graphics for plotting prices, and portfolio management. Some programs allow you to perform sophisticated fundamental and technical analyses. Investment maintenance software enables you to keep track of your investments in terms of shares, cost, and revenue. Some programs are equipped with the price and dividend history of certain securities. Investment selection software helps you decide whether to purchase or sell a stock. Investment monitoring software lets you keep track of your portfolio by using investment information in databases. You can add new prices to the files or modify old ones. Dividend information is also available. Tax investment software enables you to consider the tax aspects of certain securities. It also helps you prepare data.

Dow Jones News/Retrieval contains many databases including current and historical Dow Jones Quotes, Corporate Earnings Estimator (earnings per share estimates), Disclosure II (corporate financial statements and footnote data), Media General Financial Services (stock-performance-related ratios; comparisons-to-market indicators; bond, mutual fund, and money market information), Merrill Lynch Research Service, Weekly Economic Survey and Update (economic data, trends, and analysis), and Wall Street Highlights.

CompuServe's Executive Information Service provides financial data on companies, economic information and projections, money market trends, and earnings results and forecasts. Included are Value Line and Standard and Poor's information. CompuServe's MicroQuote provides a record of market prices, dividends, and interest paid on securities. CompuServe's mainframe will figure the worth of a portfolio for transfer to your terminal.

E. F. Hutton's *Huttonline* provides daily portfolio and account information, transaction activity, and investment research information.

Most investment programs communicate through computer terminals with outside databases such as Dow Jones News/Retrieval and various brokerage houses. To take advantage of these sources you will need a modem—a device that lets you communicate with other computers. These computerized investment programs can accommodate and track stocks, bonds, treasury securities, options, warrants, mutual funds, and commodities.

CompuStat provides twenty years of annual financial data for over 3,000 companies. Most balance sheet and income statement items are available. CompuStat tapes are compiled by Standard and Poor's.

The names and addresses of major data sources are given here. You should consider accessing these databases in order to obtain current stock and bond information.

Data Sources

Federal Sources
Federal Reserve Bank of New
    York
New York, NY 10045

Federal Reserve Bulletin
Board of Governors of the
    Federal Reserve System
Washington, DC 20551

U.S. Government Publications
Superintendent of Documents
U.S. Government Printing Office
Washington, DC 20402

Stock and Commodity Exchanges
American Stock Exchange
86 Trinity Place
New York, NY 10006

Chicago Board of Trade
LaSalle at Jackson
Chicago, IL 60604

New York Stock Exchange
11 Wall Street
New York, NY 10005

Periodicals
Business Week
1221 Avenue of Americas
New York, NY 10020

Changing Times
Kiplinger Magazine
1729 H Street, N.W.
Washington, DC 20006

Financial Analysts Journal
1633 Broadway
New York, NY 10019

Forbes
60 Fifth Avenue
New York, NY 10011

Wall Street Journal and *Barron's*
Dow Jones & Co.
Subscriptions Office
200 Burnett Road
Chicopee, MA 01021

Investment Advisory Services
Dun & Bradstreet
99 Church Street
New York, NY 10007

Moody's
99 Church Street
New York, NY 10007

Standard and Poor's
345 Hudson Street
New York, NY 10014

Value Line
Arnold Bernhard and Co.
5 East 44th St.
New York, NY 10017

Computer Data Services
CompuStat
P.O. Box 239
Denver, CO 80201

CRSP Tapes
University of Chicago
Graduate School of Business
Chicago, IL 60637

Review

1. What is the difference between a money market and a capital market?

In a money market, short-term debt securities such as six-month CDs
are traded. In a capital market, long-term securities such as stocks
and bonds are traded.

2. The capital market does not include:
    a.   municipal bonds
    b.   preferred stock
    c.   common stock
    d.   Treasury bills

    _____

    d

3. What type of securities are issued in a primary market?

    _____

    new securities

4. What kind of securities are traded in a secondary market?

    _____

    previously issued securities

5. What type of market are the organized exchanges and over-the-counter?

    _____

    secondary markets

6. **(T,F)** The listing requirements of the New York Stock Exchange and American Stock Exchange are the same.

    _____

    False. New York Stock Exchange requirements are more stringent than those of the American Stock Exchange. Many firms move on from the over-the-counter market to the American Stock Exchange to the New York Stock Exchange.

7. The _____ is the principal exchange for the future contracts of a commodity or financial instrument.

    _____

    Chicago Board of Trade

8. **(T,F)** The over-the-counter market is a centralized place for trading securities.

    _____

    False. The over-the-counter market is an informal network of dealers. Over-the-counter security transactions do not occur on an exchange.

9. How do dealers in the over-the-counter market communicate with one another?

    _____

    By means of NASDAQ, an automated system that provides bid and ask prices for over-the-counter securities.

10. In the over-the-counter market, what is meant by ask price?

_____

Ask price is the lowest price for which a dealer is willing to sell a security.

11. In the over-the-counter market, what is the dealer's spread?

_____

The dealer's spread is the difference between the bid price and the ask price. It is the dealer's profit.

12. Which is the most conservative investment strategy?
   a. high income
   b. speculation
   c. buy and hold
   d. long-term growth

_____

c

13. **(T,F)** Brokerage firms execute buy and sell orders only for securities already issued and outstanding.

_____

False. Brokerage firms also act as investment bankers in the sale of new securities. In the case of a new issue, the company obtains the funds. When outstanding securities are traded, however, the holder of the security rather than the company receives the funds. Account executives also give investors price quotations and security recommendations. Clients also receive stock and bond guides.

14. What information will you find on the monthly statement that you receive from your broker?

_____

The monthly statement includes buys, sells, commission fees, interest charges, dividend and interest income, and ending balance.

15. Why does a broker hold your stock certificates in a street name?

_____

so that he or she can buy or sell them without first obtaining your signature

16. You purchased a stock for $20 and later sold it for $24. The annual cash dividend was $1.50. How much did you earn on the investment?

_____

Dividend income	$1.50
Capital gain ($24 − $20)	4.00
Total	$5.50

17. When you purchase an investment, how soon must you pay your broker?

within five business days

18. What is a margin account?

An account in which you pay for a part of the investment and buy the remainder on credit. Your broker holds the securities as collateral and charges you interest on the money you owe.

19. In what type of brokerage account does the broker have permission to buy and sell securities at will?

discretionary account

20. Who obtains the proceeds from a short sale?

The proceeds of the short sale go to the brokerage house holding the borrowed securities in the street name.

21. What costs does the short seller have to pay?

The short seller pays commissions on both the short sale and the ultimate purchase of securities to return to the lender. The short seller also pays the dividends the lender would have received if the stock had not been loaned out. In addition, the short seller forgoes interest on the proceeds of the short sale.

22. How does the short seller earn a profit?

In a short sale, the seller hopes to sell high and buy low. If the price of the security declines, the seller earns a profit.

23. A trade of 320 shares is taken as
   a. one round lot and an odd lot
   b. a round lot
   c. three round lots and an odd lot
   d. an odd lot

c

24. What is a block trade?

a single order of at least 10,000 shares

25.   What is the danger of placing a market order?

      A market order can be executed at any price, so you might have to pay an excessively high price for a buy or accept too low a price for a sell.

26.   What is a limit order?

      an order that limits the price for which you will buy or sell a stock

27.   What is a stop-loss order?

      an order to purchase or sell a stock when its price rises to or drops below a specified amount

28.   What is a time order?

      an order to buy or sell a stock during a given time period at a specified price

29.   What fees must you pay for a sale transaction besides the broker's commission?

      state transfer taxes, federal registration fee

30.   **(T,F)** Transaction costs for stocks exceed those for bonds.

      False

31.   Prices of stocks decrease in a _____ market.

      bear

32.   What are the negative and positive aspects of the Dow Jones Industrial Average?

      The DJIA reflects the behavior of 30 blue chip stocks and hence is selective and limited. However, it does reflect the general market trend, and the securities included constitute 25% of the New York Stock Exchange value.

33.   A Dow Jones Average does *not* exist for
    a.   industrial
    b.   utilities

     c.   mutual fund
     d.   transportation

     c

34. **(T,F)** If the S & P composite stock price index declines on a particular day, it is not possible for the Dow Jones composite stock average to increase.

     False

35. Which index shows changes in the total market value of every common stock traded on the New York Stock Exchange?

     New York Stock Exchange Stock Price Index

36. Which index most often reflects the general trend of stock prices: Dow Jones Industrial Average, Standard and Poor's Stock Price Index, or New York Stock Exchange Price Index?

     New York Stock Exchange Price Index

37. In a bond quotation, the price is expressed as a percentage of _____ .

     par

38. Yield on a bond consists of _____ and _____ .

     annual interest income, capital appreciation

39. What publication provides comprehensive data about the national economy?

     Federal Reserve Bulletin

40. Name three major financial advisory services.

     Moody's, Standard and Poor's, and Value Line

41. Corporate Earnings Estimator is part of _____ .

     Dow Jones News/Retrieval

42. Value Line and Standard and Poor's information is included in
_____.

_____

CompuServe's Executive Information Service

43. A Standard and Poor's compilation in which you can find suitable stocks
is called _____.

_____

CompuStat

Self-Test

1. What is the money market?
2. What type of securities are traded in a primary market?
3. What do we call the group of investment bankers who issue new securities?
4. Future contracts are exchanged primarily on the _____.
5. What is the bid price?
6. What is the spread?
7. Which securities market trades the greatest number of issues?
8. What is the third market?
9. Match the columns.

   1. Organized exchange   A. Dealers' market
   2. Ask price minus bid price B. Direct institutional trades
   3. Over-the-counter   C. Spread
   4. NASDAQ   D. American Stock Exchange
   5. Fourth market   E. Original purchase market
   6. Primary market   F. Over-the-counter dealers' network

10. Stock certificates held by the broker are in _____ name.
11. When a stock is sold, the broker must remit the funds to the customer within how many business days?
12. Margin refers to:
    a. the maximum down payment required
    b. the minimum down payment required
    c. the maximum amount to be borrowed
    d. the basis for interest charges by the broker
13. You buy 50 shares of stock at $30 on 60% margin. The price goes to $34. What is your percentage gain?
14. In what kind of sale does the investor sell high and buy back low?
15. A trade of shares in multiples of 100 is called a _____.
16. Which order can you use to protect a profit?
    a. open order
    b. market order
    c. stop-loss order
    d. time order

17. The current price of stock is $50 a share. You place an order with your broker to buy that stock when it falls to $47. This is a
    a. limit order
    b. market order
    c. stop-loss order
    d. time order
18. **(T,F)** The transaction fees are the same to obtain a bond or stock.
19. Stock prices go up in a _____ market.
20. On what is the Dow Jones Industrial Average based?
21. Match the columns.

    1. NASDAQ Index   A.   30 blue chip stocks
    2. Value Line Average   B.   Over-the-counter stocks
    3. Dow Jones Industrial Average   C.   1,700 stocks

22. Dow Jones does not publish a(n)
    a. transportation average
    b. industrial average
    c. oil and gas average
    d. utility average
23. What are the two components of the yield on a bond?
24. Where can you find comprehensive information about the national economy?
25. Disclosure II is part of _____.
26. Standard and Poor's compilation of financial data on companies is in the _____ databases.

Self-Test Answers

1. a market in which short-term securities are traded
2. new security issuances
3. a syndicate
4. Chicago Board of Trade
5. the highest price a broker offers for a security
6. the difference between the bid price and the ask price
7. the over-the-counter market
8. a market in which securities listed on the New York Stock Exchange are bought and sold in the over-the-counter market
9. 1.   D
    2.   C
    3.   A
    4.   F
    5.   B
    6.   E
10. street
11. five
12. b

13.

Price	50 × $30	$1500
Loan	40% × $1,500	−600
Equity		$ 900

Selling price 50 × $34		$1700
Loan		−600
Equity	—	$1100

Percentage Gain:

$$\frac{\text{Gain}}{\text{Cash investment}} \quad \frac{\$200}{\$900} = 22.2\%$$

14. short sale
15. round lot
16. c
17. a
18. False
19. bull
20. The DJIA is based on 30 conservative blue chip stocks.
21. 1. B
    2. C
    3. A
22. c
23. annual interest income and capital appreciation
24. Federal Reserve Bulletin
25. Dow Jones News/Retrieval
26. CompuStat

EVALUATING RETURN AND RISK

3

Objectives

When you complete this chapter, you will be able to:

- Define return
- Differentiate between arithmetic return and geometric return
- Define risk
- Measure absolute risk and relative risk
- Identify the various risks associated with investing
- Distinguish between systematic risk and unsystematic risk
- Explain the beta coefficient

What Is Return?

Return is the reward for investing. Your return on an investment consists of periodic cash payments, called *current income*, and appreciation in market value, called *capital gain* (or capital loss if the investment depreciates).

The way you measure the return on a given investment depends primarily on the period over which you hold the investment, called the holding period. The *holding period return* (HPR) is the total return you earn from holding an investment for that period of time. It is computed as follows:

$$\text{HPR} = \frac{\text{Current income} + \text{capital gain (or loss)}}{\text{Purchase price}}$$

36

Table 3.1 shows the rates of return in ranking order by type of investment for the one-year period ended June 1985.

Table 3.1 **Rates of Return in Ranking Order as of June 1985**

Rank	Investment
1	Bonds
2	Stocks
3	U.S. Coins
4	Treasury Bills
5	Housing

Arithmetic Average Return versus Geometric Average Return

It is one thing to measure the return over a single holding period and quite another to describe a series of returns over time. When you hold an investment for more than one period, it is important to understand how to compute the average of the successive rates of return. There are two types of multiperiod average (mean) returns: *arithmetic average return* and *geometric average return*. The arithmetic return is simply the arithmetic average of successive one-period rates of return. It is defined as:

$$\text{Arithmetic return} = \frac{1}{n} \sum_{t=1}^{n} r_t$$

where n equals the number of time periods and r_t equals the single holding period return in time t. The arithmetic average return, however, can be quite misleading in multiperiod return calculations.

A more accurate measure of the actual return generated by an investment over multiple periods is the geometric average return. The geometric return over n periods is computed as follows:

$$\text{Geometric return} = n \sqrt{(1 + r_1)(1 + r_2) \ldots (1 + r_n)} - 1$$

Expected Rate of Return

You are primarily concerned with predicting future returns from an investment in a security. No one can state precisely what these future returns will be. At best you can calculate the most likely expected outcome—the expected rate of return. Of course, historical (actual) rates of return provide a useful basis for formulating these future expectations. You can use probabilities to evaluate the expected return. Using the probabilities, expected rate of return ($\bar{r}$) is the weighted average of possible returns from a given investment, weights being probabilities. Mathematically,

$$\bar{r} = \sum_{i=1}^{n} r_i p_i$$

Here r_i is the ith possible return; p_i is the probability of the ith return; and n is the number of possible returns.

Risk and the Risk-Return Trade-Off

Risk refers to the variability of possible returns associated with an investment. Risk, along with the return, is a major consideration in investment decisions. You must compare the expected return from a given investment with the risk associated with it. Higher levels of return are required to compensate for increased risk. In general, there is a wide belief in the risk-return trade-off. In other words, the higher the risk the more ample the return, and conversely, the lower the risk the more modest the return.

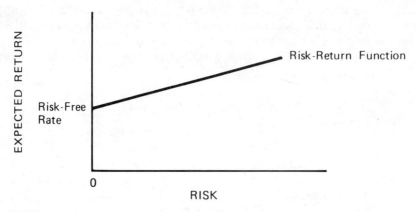

Figure 3.1   *Return versus Risk*

Measuring Risk

How do you measure your risk? Why not use the standard deviation, which is a statistical measure of dispersion of the probability distribution of possible returns. The smaller the deviation, the tighter the distribution, and thus, the lower the risk of the investment.

$$\sigma = \sqrt{\sum_{i=1}^{n}(r_i - \bar{r})^2 p_i}$$

To calculate σ, we proceed as follows:

1. Compute the expected rate of return $(\bar{r})$
2. Subtract each possible return from $\bar{r}$ to obtain a set of deviations $(r_i - \bar{r})$
3. Square each deviation, multiply the squared deviation by the probability of occurrence for its respective return, and add these products to obtain the variance (σ^2):

$$\sigma^2 = \sum_{i=1}^{n} (r_i - \bar{r})^2 p_i$$

4. Finally, take the square root of the variance to obtain the standard deviation (σ).

To follow this step-by-step approach, it is convenient to set up a table.

You must be careful in using the standard deviation to compare risk since it is only an absolute measure of dispersion (risk) and does not consider the dispersion of outcomes in relation to an expected return. In comparisons of securities with differing expected returns, we commonly use the coefficient of variation. The coefficient of variation is computed by dividing the standard deviation for a security by its expected value:

$$\frac{\sigma}{\bar{r}}$$

The higher the coefficient, the more risky the security.

Selected return rates appear in Table 3.2.

Table 3.2   **Risk and Return 1926–1978**

Series	Geometric mean	Arithmetic mean	Standard deviation
Common stocks	8.9%	11.2%	22.2%
Long-term corporate bonds	4.0%	4.1%	5.6%
Long-term government bonds	3.2%	3.4%	5.7%
U.S. Treasury bills	2.5%	2.5%	2.2%
Inflation	2.5%	2.6%	4.8%

Source: Roger G. Ibbotson and Rex A. Sinquefield, *Stocks, Bonds, Bills and Inflation: Historical Returns 1926-1978* (Charlottesville, Va.: The Financial Analysis Research Foundation, 1979) p. 12.

Types of Risk

The following sources of risk are involved in investing:

* *Business risk* is caused by fluctuations of earnings before interest and taxes (operating income). Business risk depends on variability in demand, sales

price, input prices, and amount of operating leverage. Business risk relates to the uncertainty of receiving earnings and principal from an investment.

- *Liquidity risk* represents the possibility that an asset may not be salable on short notice for its market value. An investment that must be sold at a high discount is said to have a substantial liquidity risk.
- *Default risk* is the risk that a borrower will be unable to make interest payments or principal repayments on debt. For example, there is a great amount of default risk inherent in the bonds of a company experiencing financial difficulty.
- *Market risk* refers to changes in a stock's price that result from changes in the stock market as a whole, regardless of the fundamental change in a firm's earning power. The risk may be due to political and economic uncertainties.
- *Interest rate risk* refers to the fluctuations in the value of an asset as the interest rates and conditions of the money and capital markets change. Interest rate risk relates to all investment vehicles such as fixed income securities. For example, if interest rates rise (fall), bond prices fall (rise).
- *Purchasing power risk* is related to the possibility that the investor will receive a lesser amount of purchasing power than was originally invested. Bonds are most affected by this risk since the issuer will pay back in cheaper dollars during an inflationary period. However, the return on common stock tends to move with the inflation rate.
- *Systematic risk* is nondiversifiable risk, which results from forces outside the firm's control and is therefore not unique to the given security. Purchasing power, interest rate, and market risks fall into this category.
- *Unsystematic risk* is the portion of a security's risk that can be controlled through diversification. This type of risk is unique to a given security. Business, liquidity, and default risks fall in this category.

The Beta Coefficient

There are two major types of risk associated with a security:

Total risk = systematic risk + unsystematic risk

One is the market movement or beta risk. If the market moves up or down, a stock is assumed to change in price. This type of risk is *systematic risk*, which is *nondiversifiable* or *noncontrollable*. The second type of risk, called *unsystematic risk*, indicates change in price not associated with market movement. This type of risk is unique to an individual security or industry at a given point in time and is not directly related to the market. Most of the unsystematic risk affecting a security can be diversified away in an efficiently constructed portfolio. Therefore, this type of risk does not need to be compensated with a higher level of return. The only relevant risk is systematic risk or beta risk, for which you can expect to receive compensation.

Many brokerage houses and investment services including Merrill Lynch and Value Line publish information on beta for various securities. For example, the beta for Eastman Kodak has over the years been 1.0. See Table 3.3 for betas of other companies.

Table 3.3 **"Betas" of Leading Companies***

Alcoa	1.05	General Foods	.75
AT&T	.65	General Motors	.90
Bethlehem Steel	1.25	Gulf Oil	1.15
Coca-Cola	.85	IBM	.95
Dow Chemical	1.25	Johnson & Johnson	.95
Du Pont	1.10	McDonald's	1.05
Eastman Kodak	1.00	J.C. Penney	1.00
Exxon	.90	Sears, Roebuck	.90
Ford Motor	.85	Texaco	.95
General Electric	.95	U.S. Steel	1.00

*A figure of 1.00 means price of stock usually changes about as much as the Value Line index. A stock above 1.00 is more volatile than the index.

Source: William C. Bryant, "One Way to Reduce Risk." *U.S. News & World Report*, April 19, 1982, p. 105.

Under the capital asset pricing model (CAPM), which will be covered in depth in Chapter 12, the trade-off between risk and return for an individual security is expressed through what is called the security market line (SML). The actual formula for the SML is:

$$r_j = r_f + b(r_m - r_t)$$

where r_j = the expected (or required) return on security j; r_f = the risk-free return on a security such as a Treasury bill; r_m = the expected return on the market portfolio (such as Standard and Poor's 500 Stock Composite Index or Dow Jones 30 Industrials; and b = beta, an index of systematic (nondiversifiable, noncontrollable) risk.

The key component in the CAPM, beta (b) is a measure of the security's volatility relative to an average security. For example,

b = .5 means the security is only half as volatile, or risky, as the average security

b = 1.0 means the security is of average risk

b = 2.0 means the security is twice as risky as the average risk

The whole term $b(r_m - r_t)$ represents the risk premium, the additional return above that which could be earned on, say, a Treasury bill, required to compensate you for assuming a given level of risk (as measured by beta).

Thus, the SML formula shows that the required (expected) rate of return on a given security (r_j) is equal to the return required for securities that have no risk (r_f) *plus* a risk premium required by you for assuming a given level of risk. The higher the degree of systematic risk (b), the higher the return on a given security demanded by you.

Review

1. The return on investment typically comes from two sources: _____ and capital gains.

   _____

   current income

2. The single holding period return on stock investment is _____ and capital gains or losses, divided by the _____.

   _____

   dividends, purchase price

3. Consider investments in stocks A and B over one period of ownership:

	A	B
Purchase price (beginning of year)	$100	$100
Cash dividend received (during the year)	$13	$18
Sales price (end of year)	$107	$97

   The current income from the investment in stocks A and B over the one-year period is $13 and $18, respectively. What is the capital gain (or loss) from both stocks?

   _____

   For stock A, a capital gain of $7 ($107 sales price – $100 purchase price) is realized over the period. Stock B shows a $3 capital loss ($97 sales price – $100 purchase price).

4. Combining the capital gain return (or loss) with the current income, the total return on each investment is summarized below:

Return	A	B
Current income	$13	$18
Capital gain (loss)	7	(3)
Total return	$20	$15

   Calculate the holding period return on investments A and B.

   _____

   $$\text{HPR (stock A)} = \frac{\$13 + (\$107 - \$100)}{\$100} = \frac{\$13 + \$7}{\$100}$$

   $$= \frac{\$20}{\$100} = 20\%$$

$$\text{HPR (stock B)} = \frac{\$18 + (\$97 - \$100)}{\$100} = \frac{\$18 - \$3}{\$100}$$

$$= \frac{\$15}{\$100} = 15\%$$

5. The two types of multiperiod average returns are the arithmetic return and the _____.

geometric return

6. Consider the following data where the price of a stock doubles in one period and then depreciates back to the original price. Dividend income (current income) is zero.

	Year 0	Year 1	Year 2
Price (end of period)	$80	$160	$80
HPR	—	100%	–50%

What is the arithmetic average return over the two periods?

The arithmetic average return is the average of 100% and –50%, which is 25%, as shown below:

$$\frac{100\% + (-50\%)}{2} = 25\%$$

7. In problem 6, the stock purchased for $80 and sold for the same price two periods later did not earn 25%; it clearly earned *zero* return. This can be shown be computing the geometric average return. See if you can compute this using the geometric return formula.

Note that $n = 2$, $r_1 = 100\% = 1$, and $r_2 = -50\% = -0.5$. Then,

$$\text{Geometric return} = \sqrt[2]{(1 + 1)(1 - 0.5)} - 1$$

$$= \sqrt[2]{(2)(0.5)} - 1$$

$$= \sqrt{1} - 1 = 1 - 1 = 0\%$$

8. The expected rate of return is the _____ of possible returns from a given investment, weights being _____.

weighted average, probabilities

9. Calculate the expected rate of return (r), depending upon the state of the economy, that you might earn next year on a \$50,000 investment in stock A or stock B.

STOCK A

State of economy	Return (r)	Probability (p)
Recession	−5%	.2
Normal	20	.6
Prosperity	40	.2

STOCK B

State of economy	Return (r)	Probability (p)
Recession	10%	.2
Normal	15	.6
Prosperity	20	.2

For stock A,

$$\bar{r} = (-5\%)(.2) + (20\%)(.6) + (40\%)(.2) = 19\%$$

For stock B,

$$\bar{r} = (10\%)(.2) + (15\%)(.6) + (20\%)(.2) = 15\%$$

10. _____ refers to the variability of _____ associated with a given investment.

Risk, expected return (or market price)

11. Which of the following is important in making investment decisions?
     a. risk
     b. return
     c. liquidity
     d. taxes
     e. all of the above

     e

12. As a measure of absolute risk, we use the _____.

standard deviation

13. The smaller the standard deviation, the tighter the _____ and thus, the lower the _____ of the investment.

probability distribution, risk

14. Use the step-by-step procedure to compute the standard deviation for each stock listed in problem 9.

STOCK A

Return (r_i)	Probability (p_i)	(step 1) $r_i p_i$	(step 2) $(r_i - \dot{r})$	(step 3) $(r_i - \dot{r})^2$	$(r_i - \dot{r})^2 p_i$
−5%	.2	−1%	−24%	576	115.2
20	.6	12	1	1	.6
40	.2	8	21	441	88.2
		$r = 19\%$			$\sigma^2 = 204$

(step 4) $\sigma = \sqrt{204}$
$= 14.28\%$

STOCK B

Return (r_i)	Probability (p_i)	(step 1) $r_i p_i$	(step 2) $(r_i - \dot{r})$	(step 3) $(r_i - \dot{r})^2$	$(r_i - \dot{r})^2 p_i$
10%	.2	2%	−5%	25	5
15	.6	9	0	0	0
20	.2	4	5	25	5
		$r = 15\%$			$\sigma^2 = 10$

(step 4) $\sigma = \sqrt{10}$
$= 3.16\%$

15. In comparing securities with different expected returns, we commonly use the _____.

coefficient of variation

16. (T,F) In all instances, the higher the standard deviation, the more risky the security.

False. In general, the higher the coefficient of variation, the more risky the investment. The coefficient of variation is a measure of relative risk and therefore should be used to compare securities with differing expected returns.

17. Based on the following data, compute the coefficient of variation for each stock to determine which investment is more risky.

	Stock A	Stock B
$\dot{r}$	19%	15%
σ	14.28%	3.16%

For stock A,

$$\frac{\sigma}{\bar{r}} = \frac{14.18}{19} = .75$$

For stock B,

$$\frac{\sigma}{\bar{r}} = \frac{3.16}{15} = .21$$

Although stock A produces a considerably higher return than stock B, stock A is more risky than stock B, based on the computed coefficient of variation.

18. **(T,F)** It is impossible to find a riskless investment.

True. All investments carry some degree of risk. For example, government bonds are subject to purchasing power risk and interest rate risk. Corporate bonds are also subject to business risk.

19. The best way to compensate for market risk is to
     a. keep an investment to maturity
     b. speculate
     c. obtain a loan
     d. invest in high-quality fixed-income securities like bonds and preferred stocks

     d

20. A principal advantage of common stock is that it provides a hedge against
     a. interest rate risk
     b. business risk
     c. purchasing power risk
     d. market risk

     b

21. The price of common stock may fluctuate even if there is no basic change in the company's earnings. This is called a
     a. business risk
     b. liquidity risk
     c. market risk
     d. default risk

     c

22. **(T,F)** Interest rate risk is caused by variability in yields in the money and capital markets.

_____

True

23. Which investment is most severely affected by purchasing power risk?
   a. common stock
   b. bonds
   c. preferred stock
   d. gold and silver
   e. real estate

_____

b

24. What risks are associated with U.S. Treasury bonds?

_____

purchasing power risk and interest risk

25. Total risk is the sum of _____ and _____.

_____

systematic risk, unsystematic risk

26. Unsystematic risk can be controlled through _____.

_____

diversification

27. What kinds of risk fall into the category of unsystematic risk?

_____

business, liquidity, and default risks

28. Systematic risk is measured by the _____.

_____

beta coefficient

29. The _____ formula shows that the required (or expected) rate of return on a security is equal to the risk-free rate plus _____.

_____

security market line (SML), a risk premium

30. Assume that the risk-free rate is $(r_f)=8\%$ and the expected return for the market is $(r_m)=12\%$. Calculate the required (expected) rate of return on security j if

$b = 0$
$b = .5$
$b = 1.0$
$b = 2.0$

If $b = 0$ (risk-free security) $\quad r_j = 8\% + 0(12\% - 8\%) = 8\%$
$\quad b = .5 \quad\qquad\qquad\qquad\qquad r_j = 8\% + .5(12\% - 8\%) = 10\%$
$\quad b = 1.0$ (market portfolio) $\quad r_j = 8\% + 1.0(12\% - 8\%) = 12\%$
$\quad b = 2.0 \qquad\qquad\qquad\qquad\ r_j = 8\% + 2.0(12\% - 8\%) = 16\%$

Self-Test

1. The return on common stock has two sources: _____ and
_____.

2. You purchased a share of stock for $60 a year ago and sold it today for
$65. During the year, you received four dividend payments totaling $3.60.
Compute the following:
   a.   current income
   b.   capital gain (or loss)
   c.   total return
   d.   holding period rate of return (HPR)
3. What are two kinds of multiperiod returns?
4. The percentage chance that an outcome will occur is referred to as
_____.
5. _____ is the weighted average of possible returns from a
security investment.
6. Define risk.
7. (T,F) A company with variability in revenue and expenses has greater risk.
8. _____ deviation is a measure of risk.
9. In comparing securities with differing expected returns, a useful measure
is the _____.
10. You must decide which of two securities is best for you. By using probability estimates, you have computed the following statistics:

SECURITY

	X	Y
Expected return ($\bar{r}$)	12%	8%
Standard deviation (σ)	20	10

a. Compute the coefficient of variation for each security.
b. Explain why the standard deviation and coefficient of variation give
different rankings of risk. Which method is superior and why?
11. What is market risk?
12. A U.S. Treasury bond is not subject to
   a.   any type of risk
   b.   business risk but is subject to interest rate risk

    c.   purchasing power risk but is subject to market risk

    d.   interest risk or business risk

13.   Compared to common stocks, corporate bonds are

    a.   lower in purchasing power risk but higher in business risk

    b.   lower in both business risk and purchasing power risk

    c.   higher in default risk but lower in interest rate risk

    d.   higher in both purchasing power risk and interest rate risk and subject to business risk to some degree

14.   (T,F) There is no such thing as a riskless investment.

15.   The change in yields in the money market is referred to as _____ risk.

16.   How can you minimize unsystematic risk?

17.   Assume that the risk-free rate of return is 8%, the required rate of return on the market is 13%, and stock X has a beta coefficient of 1.5.

    a.   What is stock X's required rate of return?

    b.   What will happen if the beta increases to 2.0?

    c.   What will happen if the risk-free rate decreases to 6% while the beta remains at 1.5?

18.   Describe the formula for the security market line (SML).

Self-Test Answers

1.   current income (dividend income), capital gain (or loss)

2.   a. current income = $3.60 dividend payments received

    b. capital gain = sales price – purchase price = $65 – $60 = $5

    c. total return = current income + capital gain = $3.60 + $5 = $8.60

    d. holding period rate of return $= \dfrac{\text{current income + capital gain}}{\text{purchase price}}$

$$= \frac{\$3.60 + \$5}{\$60} = \frac{\$8.60}{\$60} = 14.33\%$$

3.   arithmetic return and geometric return

4.   probability

5.   Expected return

6.   Risk is the variability in earnings (or market price).

7.   True. Variability in earnings means more uncertainty for investors and hence greater risk.

8.   Standard

9.   coefficient of variation

10.   a. The coefficient of variation is:

	X	Y
$\dfrac{\sigma}{\bar{r}}$	$\dfrac{20}{12} = 1.67$	$\dfrac{10}{8} = 1.25$

b. The coefficient of variation is a more useful measure of risk than the standard deviation because it considers the relative size of securities' expected returns. The lower the coefficient, the less risky the security relative to the expected return. Thus, security Y is relatively less risky than security X.

11. Market risk is the movement in stock price applicable to the market as a whole.

12. c

13. d

14. True

15. interest risk

16. by diversifying

17. Recall that $r_j = r_f + b(r_m - r_f)$
    a. $r_j = 8\% + 1.5(13\% - 8\%) = 15.5\%$
    b. $r_j = 8\% + 2.0(13\% - 8\%) = 18\%$
    c. $r_j = 6\% + 1.5(13\% - 6\%) = 16.5\%$

18. The security market line (SML) relates the risk measured by beta to the level of required (or expected) rate of return on a security. The formula for SML shows that the required (or expected) rate of return on a given security (r_j) is equal to the risk-free return (r_f) plus a risk premium required by investors for assuming a given level of risk. The higher the beta (an index of systematic risk), the higher the return on a given individual security demanded by investors.

FUNDAMENTAL ANALYSIS___4

Objectives

When you complete this chapter, you will be able to:

- Describe fundamental analysis
- Evaluate economic and political effects on stock price
- Consider industry factors
- Perform horizontal and vertical analysis
- Prepare financial ratios to evaluate corporate liquidity, activity, solvency, profitability, and market value
- Interpret the findings resulting from financial statement analysis
- Understand the limitations of ratio analysis
- Identify undervalued and overvalued assets and liabilities

Fundamental analysis evaluates a firm's stock based on an examination of the corporation's financial statements. It considers overall financial health, economic and political conditions, industry factors, and future outlook of the company. The analysis attempts to ascertain whether stock is overpriced, under-priced, or priced in proportion to its market value. A stock is valuable to you only if you can predict the future financial performance of the business. Financial statement analysis gives you much of the data you will need to forecast earnings and dividends.

A complete set of financial statements will include balance sheet, income statement, and statement of changes in financial position (sources and uses of funds). The first two are vital in financial statement analysis. We will discuss the various financial-statement-analysis tools that you will use in evaluating stocks and bonds. These tools include horizontal, vertical, and ratio analysis, which give a relative measure of the performance and condition of the company.

Economic and Political Considerations

Before you decide to invest in a company, you should consider that firm's economic and political risk.

Economic risk relates to the firm's ability to cope with recessions and inflations. To determine this, you should find out if the company's business is cyclical, for example, a cyclical business may not be able to pay fixed expenses in a downward economy. Earnings that are affected by cyclical activity can be unstable. Business cycles arise from three conditions: (1) changes in demand; (2) diversification of customer base; and (3) product diversification. The greater the changes in product demand, the more the company is affected by the business cycle, and thus the greater the profit variability. Diversification of customer base protects the firm because revenue is derived from industries that are affected in different ways by the business cycles. Furthermore, a company with noncyclical or countercyclical business lines has greater stability. Finally, a firm with an inadequately diversified product mix will have high correlation of income between products. The higher this correlation, the more the economic cycle will affect the business. Examples are Eastern Airlines and Chrysler. Can you think of other companies that have a high economic risk?

Political risk relates to foreign operations and governmental regulation. Multinational firms with significant foreign operations face uncertainties applying to the repatriation of funds, currency fluctuations, and foreign customs and regulations. Also, operations in politically unstable regions present risk. You should determine the company's earnings and assets in each foreign country. Two leading "problem countries" are Lebanon and Argentina. Can you think of others? Some banks, such as Citicorp, have given significant loans to risky foreign countries.

You should ascertain whether government regulation—foreign or domestic—is excessively strict. For example, a regulatory agency may try to restrain a utility from passing rate increases on to consumers, or it may refuse to approve construction of a nuclear power plant. Tight environmental and safety regulations may exist—such as stringent safety and pollution control requirements. Also consider the effect of current and proposed tax legislation on the business.

Companies that rely on government contracts and subsidies may lack stability because government spending is susceptible to changing political leadership. You should determine the percent of income a company obtains from government contracts and subsidies. One company that lost government contracts was Lockheed. Can you think of others?

Looking at the Industry

In doing a fundamental analysis, you must appraise trends in the industry of which your chosen company is a part. What is the pattern of expansion or decline in the industry? The profit dollar is worth more if earned in a healthy, expanding industry than a declining one. A firm in a rapidly changing technological industry (computers, for example) faces uncertainty due to obsolescence. A business in a staple industry has more stability because demand for its products does not fluctuate.

Capital intensive companies usually have a high degree of operating leverage (fixed cost to total cost). Examples are airlines and autos. High operating leverage magnifies changes in earnings resulting from small changes in sales leading to earnings instability. Also, risk exists because fixed costs such as rent cannot be slashed during a decline in business activity. Earnings will therefore fall off dramatically. Labor-intensive companies are generally more stable because of the variable-cost nature of the business. Variable costs such as labor can be reduced when business takes a turn for the worse.

You should examine the past and expected future stability of the industry by examining competitive forces such as ease of entry and price wars.

What industries would you stay away from and why?

Figure 4.1 shows a sequence of steps in picking a company.

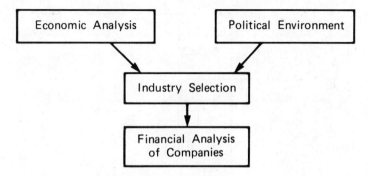

Figure 4.1   Financial Analysis Flow

Horizontal and Vertical Analysis

Horizontal analysis concentrates on the trend in the accounts in dollar and percentage terms over the years. It is typically presented in comparative financial statements (see Figures 4.2 and 4.3). In annual reports, comparative financial data are usually shown for five years. Through horizontal analysis you can pinpoint areas of wide divergence requiring investigation.

In the income statement shown in Figure 4.3, the significant rise in sales returns taken with the reduction in sales for 19XB–19XC should cause concern. You might compare these results with those of competitors. The problem might be with the industry in general or with the company.

It is essential to present both the dollar amount of change and the percentage of change since the use of one without the other may result in erroneous conclusions. The interest expense from 19XA–19XB went up by 100.0%, but this represented only $1,000 and may not need further investigation. In a similar vein, a large number change might cause a small percentage change and not be of any great importance.

In *vertical analysis*, a material financial statement item is used as a base value, and all other accounts on the financial statement are compared to it.

Jones Inc.
Comparative Balance Sheet (In Thousands of Dollars)
December 31, 19XC, 19XB, 19XA

	19XC ①	19XB ②	19XA ③	Increase or Decrease 19XC – 19XB (Increase ④ / Decrease ⑤)		Increase or Decrease 19XB – 19XA (Increase ⑥ / Decrease ⑦)		Percent Increase or Decrease 19XC – 19XB ⑧	Percent Increase or Decrease 19XB – 19XA ⑨
ASSETS									
Current Assets:									
Cash	$ 28	$ 36	$ 36		(8)			(22.2%)	—
Accounts Receivable	21	16	10	5		6		31.3	500%
Marketable Securities	22	15	7	7		8		46.7	114.3
Inventory	53	46	49	7			(3)	15.2	(6.1)
Total Current Assets	$ 124	$ 113	$ 102	11		11		9.7	10.8
Plant Assets	103	91	83	12		8		13.2	9.6
Total Assets	$ 227	$ 204	$ 185	23		19		11.3	10.3
LIABILITIES									
Current Liabilities	$ 56	$ 50	$ 51	6			(1)	12.0	(2.0)
Long-term Liabilities	83	74	69	9		5		12.2	7.2
Total Liabilities	$ 139	$ 124	$ 120	15		4		12.1	3.3
STOCKHOLDERS' EQUITY									
Common Stock, $10 par, 4,600 shares	$ 46	$ 46	$ 46					—	—
Retained Earnings	42	34	19	8		15		23.5	78.9
Total Stockholders' Equity	$ 88	$ 80	$ 65	8		15		10.0	23.1
Total Liabilities and Stockholders' Equity	$ 227	$ 204	$ 185	23		19		11.3	10.3

Figure 4.2   Jones Company: Comparative Balance Sheet

Jones Inc.
Comparative Income Statement (In Thousands of Dollars) ①

	For the Years Ended Dec. 31, 19XC, 19XB, 19XA	19XC ②	19XB ③	19XA ④	Increase or Decrease 19XC - 19XB ⑤	Decrease 19XB - 19XA ⑥	Percent Increase or Decrease 19XC - 19XB ⑥	19XB - 19XA ⑦
1	Sales	$ 983.0	$ 1200.0	$ 566.6	$ (21.7)	$ 63.4	18.1%	112.0%
2	Sales Returns & Allowances	18.0	10.0	4.0	8	6	80.0	150.0
3	Net Sales	$ 803.0	$ 1100.0	$ 526.6	$ (29.7)	$ 57.4	(27.0)	109.1
4	Cost of Goods Sold	520.0	630.0	280.0	(11.0)	35.0	(17.5)	125.0
5	Gross Profit	$ 283.0	$ 470.0	$ 246.6	$ (18.7)	$ 29.4	(39.8)	91.1
6	Operating Expenses							
7	Selling Expenses	$ 12.0	$ 13.0	$ 11.0	$ (1)	$ 2	(7.7)	18.2
8	General Expenses	5.0	8.0	3.0	(3)	5	(37.6)	166.7
9	Total Operating Expenses	$ 17.0	$ 21.0	$ 14.0	$ (4)	$ 7	(19.0)	50.0
10								
11	Income from Operations	$ 113.0	$ 260.0	$ 106.6	$ (14.7)	$ 15.4	(56.5)	145.3
12	Nonoperating Income	4.0	1.0	2.0	3	(1)	300.0	(50.0)
13	Income before Interest Expense & Taxes	$ 153.0	$ 270.0	$ 126.6	$ (11.7)	$ 14.4	(43.3)	114.3
14	Interest Expense	20.0	20.0	1.0	—	1.0	100.0	100.0
15	Income before Taxes	$ 133.0	$ 250.0	$ 116.6	$ (11.7)	$ 13.4	(46.8)	115.5
16	Income Taxes (40% rate)	53.0	100.0	46.6	(4.7)	5.4	(47.0)	117.4
17	Net Income	$ 80.0	$ 150.0	$ 70.0	$ (70)	$ 8.0	46.7	114.3

Figure 4.3   Jones Company: Comparative Income Statement

In the balance sheet, for example, total assets equal 100%. Each asset is stated as a percentage of total assets. Similarly, total liabilities and stockholders' equity is assigned 100% with a given liability or equity account stated as a percentage of the total liabilities and stockholders' equity. For the income statement, 100% is assigned to net sales with all other revenue and expense accounts related to it.

Under vertical analysis, the statements showing the percentages are referred to as common size statements. You should compare common size percentages from one period to another to identify areas that need attention.

Vertical analysis depicts the company's internal structure and reveals the relative amount of each income statement account to revenue. It presents the asset mix that generates income and the mix of the sources of funds.

You should compare the vertical percentages of the business to those of the competition and to the industry norms. Then you can determine the company's relative position.

Figure 4.4 shows a common size income statement based on the data provided in Figure 4.3.

Ratio Analysis

Horizontal and vertical analysis compares one figure to another within the same category. It is also vital to compare two figures applicable to different categories. This is accomplished by *ratio analysis*. In selecting the base year for your analysis, you should choose the most representative year of corporate performance.

To obtain useful conclusions from the ratios, you must make two comparisons:

- *Industry comparison.* You must compare the company's ratios to those of competing companies in the industry or with industry standards (averages). You can obtain industry norms from financial services such as Value Line, Dun and Bradstreet, and Standard and Poor's.
- *Trend analysis.* Here you will compare a given ratio for one company over several years to see the direction of financial health or operational performance.

Financial ratios include liquidity, asset utilization (activity), solvency (leverage), profitability, and market value.

Liquidity

Liquidity is the firm's ability to satisfy maturing short-term debt. Liquidity is crucial to carrying out the business, especially during periods of adversity. It relates to the short term, typically a period of one year or less. Poor liquidity might lead to lower market price of stock, higher cost of financing, and inability to pay dividends.

Throughout our discussion, keep referring to the figures to make sure you understand where the numbers come from.

Jones Inc.
Income Statement and Common Size Analysis

(In Thousands of Dollars)

For the Years Ended
December 31, 19XC & 19XB

		19XC		19XB	
		Amount ①	Percent ②	Amount ③	Percent ④
1	Sales	$ 98.3	122.4%	$ 120.0	109.1%
2	Sales Returns & Allowances	18.0	22.4	10.0	9.1
3	Net Sales	$ 80.3	100.0	$ 110.0	100.0
4	Cost of Goods Sold	52.0	64.8	63.0	57.3
5	Gross Profit	$ 28.3	35.2	$ 47.0	42.7
6	Operating Expenses				
7	Selling Expenses	$ 12.0	14.9	$ 13.0	11.8
8	General Expenses	5.0	6.2	8.0	7.3
9	Total Operating Expenses	$ 17.0	21.1	$ 21.0	19.1
10	Income from Operations	$ 11.3	14.1	$ 26.0	23.6
11	Nonoperating Income	4.0	5.0	1.0	1.0
12	Income before Interest				
13	Expense and Taxes	$ 15.3	19.1	$ 27.0	24.6
14	Interest Expense	2.0	2.5	2.0	1.8
15	Income before Taxes	$ 13.3	16.6	$ 25.0	22.8
16	Income Taxes	5.3	6.6	10.0	9.1
17	Net Income	$ 8	10.0	$ 15.0	13.7

Figure 4.4   Jones Company: Income Statement and Common Size Analysis

Net working capital equals current assets minus current liabilities. Net working capital for 19XC is:

$$\text{Net working capital} = \text{current assets} - \text{current liabilities}$$
$$= \$124 - \$56$$
$$= \$68$$

In 19XB, net working capital was $63. The rise over the year is favorable.

The *current ratio* equals current assets divided by current liabilities. The ratio reflects the company's ability to satisfy current debt from current assets.

$$\text{Current ratio} = \frac{\text{current assets}}{\text{current liabilities}}$$

For 19XC, the current ratio is:

$$\frac{\$124}{\$56} = 2.21$$

In 19XB, the current ratio was 2.26. The ratio's decline over the year points to a slight reduction in liquidity.

The *acid-test ratio* is a stringent liquidity test:

$$\text{Acid-test ratio} = \frac{\text{cash} + \text{marketable securities} + \text{accounts receivable}}{\text{current liabilities}}$$

The quick ratio for 19XC is:

$$\frac{\$28 + \$21 + \$22}{\$56} = 1.27$$

In 19XB, the ratio was 1.34. A small reduction in the ratio over the period points to less liquidity.

The overall liquidity trend shows a slight deterioration as reflected in the lower current and quick ratios. But a mitigating factor is the increase in net working capital.

Asset Utilization

Asset utilization (activity, turnover) ratios examine how soon given accounts are converted to sales or cash. One example is the speed with which the company turns over receivables, inventory, and fixed assets. Activity ratios reflect the way in which a company uses its assets to obtain revenue and profit. The higher the turnover, the more efficiently the business manages its assets.

Accounts receivable ratios comprise the accounts receivable turnover and the number of days receivables are held. The *accounts receivable turnover* provides the number of times accounts receivable are collected in the year. It is derived by dividing net credit sales by average accounts receivable. You can calculate average accounts receivable by adding the beginning and ending accounts receivable and dividing by 2.

$$\text{Accounts receivable turnover} = \frac{\text{net credit sales}}{\text{average accounts receivable}}$$

For 19XC, the average accounts receivable is:

$$\frac{\$21 + \$16}{2} = \$18.5$$

The accounts receivable turnover for 19XC is:

$$\frac{\$80.3}{\$18.5} = 4.34$$

In 19XB, the turnover was 8.46. There is a sharp reduction in the turnover rate pointing to a material collection problem. Perhaps the company's credit policy is deficient?

The *average collection period* is the length of time it takes to collect receivables.

$$\text{Average collection period} = \frac{365}{\text{accounts receivable turnover}}$$

In 19XC, the collection period is:

$$\frac{365}{4.34} = 84.1 \text{ days}$$

It takes this firm about 84 days to convert receivables to cash. In 19XB, the collection period was 43.1 days. The significant lengthening of the collection period points to an increase in the realization risk in receivables.

Inventory ratios are useful when a buildup in inventory exists. This ties up cash flow and can result in lost opportunities for profit as well as increased storage costs. Before you invest or reinvest, you should examine the company's inventory turnover and average age of inventory.

$$\text{Inventory turnover} = \frac{\text{cost of goods sold}}{\text{average inventory}}$$

The inventory turnover for 19XC is:

$$\frac{\$52}{\$49.5} = 1.05$$

For 19XB, the turnover was 1.33.

$$\text{Average age of inventory} = \frac{365}{\text{inventory turnover}}$$

In 19XC, the average age was:

$$\frac{365}{1.05} = 347.6 \text{ days}$$

In the previous year, the average age was 274.4 days.

The reduction in the turnover and increase in inventory age points to a longer holding of inventory, which could lead to obsolescence. Why is the inventory not selling as quickly?

The *operating cycle* is the number of days it takes to convert inventory and receivables to cash.

$$\text{Operating cycle} = \text{average collection period} + \text{average age of inventory}$$

In 19XC, the operating cycle is:

$$84.1 \text{ days} + 347.6 \text{ days} = 431.7 \text{ days}$$

In the previous year, the operating cycle was 317.5 days. An unfavorable direction is indicated because additional funds are tied up in noncash assets. Cash is being collected more slowly.

By calculating the *total asset turnover*, you can find out whether the company is efficiently employing its total assets to obtain revenue. A low ratio may indicate too high an investment in assets in comparison to the sales revenue generated.

$$\text{Total asset turnover} = \frac{\text{net sales}}{\text{average total assets}}$$

In 19XC, the ratio is:

$$\frac{\$80.3}{\$215.5} = .37$$

In 19XB, the ratio was .57 ($110/$194.5). There has been a sharp reduction in asset utilization.

This company has suffered a sharp deterioration in activity ratios, pointing to a need for improved credit and inventory management. Additional problems are inefficient collection and obsolescence of inventory.

Solvency

Solvency is the company's ability to satisfy long-term debt as it becomes due. You should be concerned about the long-term financial and operating structure of any firm in which you might invest. Another important consideration is the size of debt in the firm's capital structure, which is referred to as *financial leverage*. Solvency also depends on earning power; in the long run a company will not satisfy its debts unless it earns profit.

A leveraged capital structure subjects the company to fixed interest charges, which contributes to earnings instability. Excessive leverage makes it difficult for the firm to meet interest payments and principal at maturity. It also can cause the company to run out of cash under adverse conditions. Excessive debt may also make it difficult for the firm to borrow funds at reasonable rates during tight money markets.

The *debt ratio* reveals the amount of money a company owes to its creditors. Excessive debt means greater risk to the investor. (Remember that equity holders come after creditors in bankruptcy.) The debt ratio is:

$$\frac{\text{Total liabilities}}{\text{Total assets}}$$

In 19XC, the ratio is:

$$\frac{\$139}{\$227} = .61$$

In 19XB, the ratio was .61. Creditor interest in the firm has remained constant.

The *debt-equity ratio* will show you if the firm has a great amount of debt in its capital structure. Large debts mean that the borrower has to pay significant periodic interest and principal. Also, a heavily indebted firm takes a greater risk of running out of cash in difficult times. This ratio depends on several variables, including the rates of other firms in the industry, the degree of access to additional debt financing, and stability of operations.

The ratio equals:

$$\frac{\text{Total liabilities}}{\text{Stockholders' equity}}$$

In 19XC, the ratio is:

$$\frac{\$139}{\$88} = 1.58$$

In the previous year, the ratio was 1.55. The trend is relatively static.

Interest coverage ratio (times interest earned) tells you how many times the firm's before-tax earnings would cover interest. It is a safety margin indicator in that it reflects how much of a reduction in earnings a company can tolerate.

$$\frac{\text{Income before interest and taxes}}{\text{Interest expense}}$$

For 19XC, the ratio is:

$$\frac{\$15.3}{\$2.0} = 7.65$$

In 19XB, interest was covered 13.5 times. The reduction in coverage during the period is a bad sign. It means that less earnings are now available to satisfy interest charges.

You must also account for *undervalued liabilities* in the balance sheet by closely examining footnote disclosure. For example, you should find out about lawsuits, noncapitalized leases, and future guarantees.

Unrecorded assets indicate improved financial health; so do *undervalued assets*. Examples are a tax loss carry-forward benefit, a purchase commitment in which the contract price is less than the current price, and the value of human resources.

The company's overall solvency has remained fairly constant. There has been no significant change in its ability to satisfy long-term debt. Significantly less profit is available to cover interest payments, however.

Profitability

A company's ability to earn a good profit and return on investment is an indicator of its financial well-being and the efficiency with which it is managed. Poor earnings have detrimental effects on market price of stock and dividends. Total dollar net income has little meaning unless it is compared to the input in getting that profit.

The *gross profit margin* shows the percentage of each dollar remaining once the company has paid for goods acquired. A high margin reflects good earning potential.

$$\text{Gross profit margin} = \frac{\text{gross profit}}{\text{net sales}}$$

In 19XC, the ratio is:

$$\frac{\$28.3}{\$80.3} = .35$$

The ratio was .43 in 19XB. The reduction shows that the company now receives less profit on each dollar sales. Perhaps higher relative cost of merchandise sold is at fault.

Profit margin shows the earnings generated from revenue and a key indicator of operating performance. It gives you an idea of the firm's pricing, cost structure, and production efficiency.

$$\text{Profit margin} = \frac{\text{net income}}{\text{net sales}}$$

The ratio in 19XC is:

$$\frac{\$8}{\$80.3} = .10$$

For the previous year, profit margin was .14. The decline in the ratio shows a downward trend in earning power.

Return on investment is a prime indicator because it allows you to evaluate the profit you will earn if you invest in the business. Two key ratios are the *return on total assets* and the *return on stockholders' investment.*

The return on total assets shows whether management is efficient in using available resources to get profit.

$$\text{Return on total assets} = \frac{\text{net income}}{\text{average total assets}}$$

In 19XC, the return is:

$$\frac{\$8}{(\$227 + \$204)/2} = .037$$

In 19XB, the return was .077. There has been a deterioration in the productivity of assets in generating earnings.

The *return on common equity* reflects the rate of return earned on common stockholders' investment.

$$\text{Return on common equity} = \frac{\text{earnings available to common stockholders}}{\text{average stockholders' equity}}$$

The return in 19XC is:

$$\frac{\$8}{(\$88 + \$80)/2} = 0.95$$

In 19XB, the return was .207. There has been a significant drop in return to the owners.

The overall profitability of the company has decreased considerably, causing a decline in both the return on assets and return on equity. Perhaps lower earnings were due in part to higher costs of short-term financing arising from the decline in the liquidity and activity ratios. Moreover, as turnover rates in assets go down, profit will similarly decline because of a lack of sales and higher costs of carrying higher current asset balances.

Table 4.1 **Industries with High Return on Equity Rates**

Aerospace
Broadcasting
Drugs
Food Processing
Office Equipment
Paper

Market Value

Market value ratios relate the company's stock price to its earnings (or book value) per share. Also included are dividend-related ratios.

Earnings Per Share (EPS) is the ratio most widely watched by investors. EPS reflects the net income per share owned. For preferred stock, you reduce net income by the preferred dividends to obtain the amount of earnings available to common stock holders. Where preferred stock is not in the capital structure, you determine EPS by dividing net income by common shares outstanding. EPS is a gauge of corporate operating performance and of expected future dividends.

$$EPS = \frac{\text{net income – preferred dividend}}{\text{common shares outstanding}}$$

EPS in 19XC is:

$$\frac{\$8,000}{4,600 \text{ shares}} = \$1.74$$

For 19XB, EPS was $3.26. The sharp reduction over the year should cause alarm among investors.

Table 4.2 **Highly Profitable Companies**

Abbott Laboratories
Ames Dept. Stores
Capital Cities
International Business Machines
Pfizer, Inc.

The *price/earnings ratio* (P/E) reflects the company's relationship to its stockholders. A high multiple is favorable since it shows that investors view the firm positively. On the other hand, some prefer a relatively lower multiple as compared with companies of similar risk and return.

$$\text{Price/earnings ratio} = \frac{\text{market price per share}}{\text{earnings per share}}$$

Assume a market price per share of $12 on December 31, 19XC, and $26 on December 31, 19XB. The P/E ratios are:

19XC: $\dfrac{\$12}{\$1.74} = 6.90$

19XB: $\dfrac{\$26}{\$3.26} = 7.98$

From the lower P/E multiple, you can infer that the stock market now has a lower opinion of the business. However, some investors argue that a low P/E ratio can mean that the stock is undervalued. Nevertheless, the decline over the year in stock price was 54% ($14/$26), which should cause deep investor concern.

Table 4.3 shows price-earnings ratios of certain companies.

Table 4.3   **P/E Ratios**

Company	Industry	1984
Marriott	Hotel	14
R.J. Reynolds	Tobacco	9
Union Camp	Timber	10
Westinghouse	Electronics	8

Book value per share is the net assets available to common stock holders divided by shares outstanding. By comparing it to market price per share you can get another view of how investors feel about the business.

The book value per share in 19XC is:

$$\frac{\text{Total stockholders' equity} - \text{preferred stock}}{\text{Common shares outstanding}}$$

$$\frac{\$88,000 - 0}{4,600} = \$19.13$$

In 19XB, book value per share was $17.39.

The increased book value per share is a favorable sign, because it indicates that each share now has a higher book value. However, in 19XC, market price is much less than book value, and that is a very negative sign. During inflation, current market price should exceed historical cost. This means that the stock market does not value the security highly. In 19XB, market price *did* exceed book value, but there is now some doubt in the minds of stockholders concerning the company. However, some analysts may argue that the stock is underpriced.

The *price/book value ratio* shows the market value of the company in comparison to its historical accounting value. A company with old assets may have a high ratio whereas one with new assets may have a low ratio. Hence, when you examine the meaning of the changes in the ratio, you should appraise the corporate assets and industry norms. The ratio equals:

$$\frac{\text{Market price per share}}{\text{Book value per share}}$$

In 19XC, the ratio is:

$$\frac{\$12}{\$19.13} = .63$$

In 19XB, the ratio was 1.5. The significant drop in the ratio may indicate a lower opinion of the company in the eyes of investors. Market price of stock may have dropped because of a deterioration in liquidity, activity, and profitability ratios. The major indicators of a company's performance are intertwined—one affects the other—so that problems in one area may spill over into another. This appears to have happened to the company in our example.

Dividend ratios help you determine the current income from an investment. Two relevant ratios are:

$$\text{Dividend yield} = \frac{\text{dividends per share}}{\text{market price per share}}$$

$$\text{Dividend payout} = \frac{\text{dividends per share}}{\text{earnings per share}}$$

Stockholders look unfavorably upon reduced dividends because dividend payout is a sign of the financial health of the business.

Table 4.4 shows the dividend payout ratios of some companies.

Table 4.4 **Dividend Payout Ratios, 1984**

Mobil	71%
Philip Morris	45%
R.H. Macy	21%

Limitations of Ratio Analysis

Trends in ratios are useful in security analysis, but you must also recognize the following limitations:

1. Accounting policies vary among companies and can inhibit useful comparisons. For example, the use of different depreciation methods (straight-line vs. double declining balance) will affect profitability and return ratios.
2. The accounting measurement process ignores inflation.
3. Management may "fool around" with ("window-dress") the figures. For example, it can reduce needed research expense just to bolster net income.
4. A ratio is *static* and does not reveal future flows. How much cash do you have in your pocket *now*? Is that sufficient, considering your expenses and income over the next month?
5. A ratio does not indicate the quality of its components. For example, a high quick ratio may contain risky receivables.
6. Reported assets may be undervalued. One example is a patent recorded at its registration price even though it could generate enormous future cash flow.
7. Reported assets such as obsolete merchandise may be overvalued.
8. Reported liabilities may be undervalued—failure to properly book a lawsuit, for instance.
9. Liabilities may be overstated. A convertible bond with an attractive conversion feature, for example, could later be converted to stock.
10. Accounting involves many estimates such as the expected life of an asset or the percent of anticipated uncollectible accounts on receivables.
11. The company may have multiple lines of business, making it difficult to identify the industry group of which the company is a part.
12. Industry averages cited by financial advisory services are only approximations. Hence, you may have to compare a company's ratios to those of competing companies in the industry.

As you can see, financial statement analysis requires more than merely computing ratios. It involves an evaluation of all the factors bearing on the financial health of the company.

Review

1. What is fundamental analysis?

　　　　an appraisal of the financial performance of a business undertaken in an attempt to predict earnings and risk, based on economic, political, and industry considerations

2. How is technical analysis different from fundamental analysis?

　　　　Technical analysis allows one to predict future prices by studying past price, volume, and other information.

3. What must you consider in appraising the effects of economic developments on the business?

impact of recession and inflation, degree of cyclicality, elasticity of product demand, and diversification in the product and customer base

4. What industry factors should you consider?

degree of growth or contraction, technological nature, capital or labor intensive, stability of product demand, and competitive nature

5. What is meant by operating leverage? Is a high ratio good or bad?

$$\frac{\text{Fixed cost}}{\text{Total cost}}$$

A high ratio is bad.

6. _____ compares an account to the same account of an earlier period.

Horizontal analysis

7. In a common size income statement, _____ is assigned the value of 100.

net sales

8. A corporation gives the following comparative income for a two-year period:

	19X2	19X1
Sales	$540	$700
Cost of goods sold	220	200
Gross profit	$320	$500
Operating expenses	105	195
Earnings before interest and taxes	$215	$305

a. Using horizontal analysis, find the percentage change.
b. Appraise the resulting information.

a.

Percent Change
(22.9%)
10.0
(36.0)
(46.2)
(29.5)

b. Gross profit went down by 36.0% because of the effect of a lower sales base and increased cost of sales. But operating expenses were cost controlled so that the profit reduction was less pronounced.

9. Another company presented the following income statement information:

	19X2	19X1
Net sales	$420	$260
Cost of goods sold	270	140
Operating expenses	60	48

a. Using vertical analysis prepare comparative common size income statements.
b. Appraise the findings.

a.

	19X2		19X1	
	Amount	Percent	Amount	Percent
Net sales	$420	100.0%	$260	100.0%
Cost of goods sold	270	64.3	140	53.8
Gross profit	$150	35.7	$120	46.2
Operating expenses	60	14.3	48	18.5
EBIT	$ 90	21.4	$ 72	27.7

b. Cost of sales has increased perhaps because of the higher cost of buying goods. Cost control over expenses is indicated. However, the bottom line has deteriorated.

10. In financial ratio analysis, what year should you use as the base year?
   a. the first year selected for analysis
   b. the year most typical of business activity
   c. no year
   d. the last year selected for analysis

   b

11. After you have determined a company's ratios for the current year, what should you compare them to?

   previous year ratios, competitive company ratios, and industry norms

12. _____ is the ability of a business to satisfy current liabilities out of current assets.

   Liquidity

13. _____ is in the current ratio but not the quick ratio.

Inventory

14. Does a profitable business necessarily have a good liquidity position?

No. Profitability does not always mean liquidity. For example, earnings may be high but revenue may not be in cash.

15. In evaluating the liquidity of a seasonal business, do the year-end balances necessarily indicate liquidity?

No. You have to analyze liquidity during different times of the year. The year-end liquidity position may not reflect what is typical.

16. The failure of a company to take advantage of cash discounts on the early payment to creditors is a sign of poor _____.

liquidity

17. What are the implications of a significant rise in the ratios of fixed assets to short-term debt and short-term debt to long-term debt?

An increase in these ratios may indicate a serious financial problem. If a company finances long-term assets with short-term obligations, it will not realize a return from these assets before the debt matures. The firm has liquidity risk if it has insufficient funds to satisfy the short-term obligations.

18. Use the partial balance sheet that follows to compute the answers to questions a, b, c, and d, below.

Current assets:

Cash	$3,500
Marketable securities	7,000
Accounts receivable	95,000
Inventories	110,000
Prepaid expenses	500
Total current assets	$216,000
Fixed assets	$680,000

Current liabilities:

Notes payable	$ 4,000
Accounts payable	125,000
Accrued expenses	26,000
Total current liabilities	$155,000

Long-term liabilities $400,000

The industry norm for the current ratio is 2:3, and the quick-ratio norm is 1:2.

a. Compute net working capital.
b. Compute current ratio.
c. Compute quick ratio.
d. Evaluate the company on the basis of your calculations.

---

a. Net working capital = current assets – current liabilities
= $216,000 – $155,000
= $61,000

b. Current ratio = $\dfrac{\text{current assets}}{\text{current liabilities}} = \dfrac{\$216,000}{\$155,000} = 1.39$

c. Quick ratio = $\dfrac{\text{cash + marketable securities + accounts receivable}}{\text{current liabilities}}$

$= \dfrac{\$105,500}{\$155,000} = .68$

d. The company's liquidity is poor, since the current ratio and quick ratio are below the industry norms. Also, as a general rule, the current ratio should be at least 2:1, and the quick ratio should be at least 1:1.

19. The _____ equals the number of days inventory is held plus the number of days receivables are held.

---

operating cycle

20. Use these accounts receivable figures to answer a and b.

	19X2	19X1
Average accounts receivable	$385	$420
Net credit sales	$2,500	$3,400

The terms of sale are 45 days.

a. Determine the accounts-receivable turnover and the number of days receivables are held.
b. What analytical conclusions can you draw?

---

a.

	19X2	**19X1**
Accounts receivable turnover	$\dfrac{\$2,500}{\$385} = 6.49$	$\dfrac{\$3,400}{\$420} = 8.10$
Collection period	$\dfrac{365}{6.49} = 56.24$ days	$\dfrac{365}{8.10} = 45.06$ days

b. The direction of the firms accounts-receivable management is negative. In 19X2, the collection period was longer than the term of sale. There was a sizable lengthening of the collection period over the year, pointing to possible cash flow problems. Perhaps a problem exists in the credit department.

21. On January 1, 19X3, Scott Company's inventory was $380. During the year, the firm made purchases of $1,700. On December 31, 19X3, the inventory stood at $450.

a. Compute the inventory turnover and number of days inventory is held for 19X3.

b. Assuming an inventory turnover in 19X2 of 2.9 and an average of inventory of 106 days, evaluate the results for 19X3.

---

a. Cost of goods sold:

Beginning inventory	$380
Purchases	1,700
Cost of goods available	$2,080
Ending inventory	450
Cost of goods sold	$1,630

$$\text{Average inventory} = \frac{\text{beginning inventory} + \text{ending inventory}}{2}$$

$$= \frac{\$380 + \$450}{2} = \$415$$

$$\text{Inventory turnover} = \frac{\text{cost of goods sold}}{\text{average inventory}} = \frac{\$1,630}{\$415} = 3.93$$

$$\text{Number of days inventory is held} = \frac{365}{\text{inventory turnover}}$$

$$\frac{365}{3.93} = 92.88 \text{ days}$$

b. The company's inventory management improved in 19X3 as shown by the increased turnover rate and the decreased age of inventory. Less liquidity risk exists. Also, as inventory moves more quickly, profit will increase.

22. _____ leverage relates to the ratio of debt to equity.

Financial

23. What is one ratio you can use to compute the degree of financial leverage?

$$\frac{\text{Total liabilities}}{\text{Total stockholders' equity}}$$

24. The interest coverage ratio equals _____ divided by _____.

income before interest and tax, interest

25. You can determine return on owners' equity by dividing _____ by _____.

net income, average stockholders' equity

26. Use these financial data to answer the questions that follow:
Balance sheet data as of December 31, 19X1:

Assets

Current assets	$105
Fixed assets	160
Total assets	$265

Liabilities and stockholders' equity:

Current liabilities	$120
Long-term liabilities	85
Total liabilities	$205
Stockholders' equity	60
Total liabilities and stockholders' equity	$265

Income statement data:

Net sales	$390
Interest expense	3
Net income	24

Account balances as of December 31, 19X0:

Total assets	$210
Stockholders' equity	50

Industry norms at December 31, 19X1:

Debt/equity ratio	1.8
Profit margin	.14
Return on total assets	.16
Return on stockholders' equity	.37
Total asset turnover	1.94

Determine and appraise the following ratios on December 31, 19X1:
a.   Debt/equity ratio
b.   Profit margin
c.   Return on total assets
d.   Return on stockholders' equity
e.   Total asset turnover

---

a. $\dfrac{\text{Total liabilities}}{\text{Stockholders' equity}} = \dfrac{\$205}{\$60} = 3.42$

The debt/equity ratio significantly exceeds the industry norm. Hence, a solvency problem exists. High debt makes it hard for the company to satisfy debt when business activity fails. The firm will also have difficulty borrowing in a stringent money market.

b.   Profit margin $= \dfrac{\text{net income}}{\text{net sales}} = \dfrac{\$24}{\$390} = .06$

The profit margin trails the industry average, and this tells you that the company's operating performance is deficient.

c.   Return on total assets $= \dfrac{\text{net income}}{\text{average total assets}} = \dfrac{\$24}{\$237.5} = .10$

The return rate is below the industry norm. Hence, asset efficiency in obtaining earnings is unsatisfactory.

d.   Return on stockholders' equity $= \dfrac{\text{net income}}{\text{average stockholders' equity}}$

$= \dfrac{\$24}{\$55} = .44$

The return to stockholders is better than the industry average, showing that investment in this company is better than investment in competing firms. Perhaps this is the result of the firm's use of leverage (or debt).

e. $\dfrac{\text{Net sales}}{\text{Average total assets}} = \dfrac{\$390}{\$237.5} = 1.64$

The asset turnover is below industry standard, showing an inability to utilize assets in deriving revenue. The poor asset utilization may be a reason for the poor profit margin and return on total assets.

27. The price/earnings ratio equals _____ divided by _____.

_____

market price per share, earnings per share

28. Two measures of interest to stockholders in appraising the dividend policy of a company are the dividend _____ and dividend _____.

_____

yield, payout

29. What can the investor probably conclude when book value per share is higher than market price per share?

_____

The stock market does not think much of the firm. Perhaps the company has financial problems. In inflation, market price per share should be greater than book value per share. (However, some believe that this is an indication the stock is undervalued.)

30. Use these financial statements to answer the questions that follow.

Balance Sheet
December 31, 19X1

Assets
Current Assets:

Cash	$ 95	
Marketable securities	210	
Inventory	320	
Total current assets		$625
Plant assets		520
Total assets		$1,145

Liabilities and stockholders' equity

Current liabilities	$210	
Long-term liabilities	105	
Total liabilities		$ 315
Stockholders' equity:		
Common stock, $1 par value, 105,000 shares	$105	
Premium on common stock	450	
Retained earnings	275	
Total stockholders' equity		830
Total liabilities and stockholders' equity		$1,145

Income Statement
Year Ended December 31, 19X1

Net sales	$10,200
Cost of sales	6,300
Gross profit	$ 3,900
Operating expenses	850
Income before taxes	$ 3,050
Income taxes (46% rate)	1,403
Net income	$ 1,647

Additional data:

Market price per share	$140
Total dividends	620
Beginning inventory	225

Determine each of the following ratios:
a. Current ratio
b. Quick ratio
c. Inventory turnover
d. Age of inventory
e. Debt/equity ratio
f. Book value per share
g. Earnings per share
h. Price/earnings ratio
i. Dividends per share
j. Dividend payout
k. Debt ratio

---

a. $$\text{Current ratio} = \frac{\text{current assets}}{\text{current liabilities}} = \frac{\$625}{\$210} = 2.98$$

b. $$\text{Quick ratio} = \frac{\text{cash + marketable securities}}{\text{current liabilities}} = \frac{\$305}{\$210} = 1.45$$

c. $$\text{Inventory turnover} = \frac{\text{cost of goods sold}}{\text{average inventory}} = \frac{\$6,300}{\$272.5} = 23.12$$

d. $$\text{Age of inventory} = \frac{365}{\text{inventory turnover}} = \frac{365}{23.12} = 15.79$$

e. $$\text{Debt/equity} = \frac{\text{total liabilities}}{\text{stockholders' equity}} = \frac{\$315}{\$830} = .38$$

f. Book value = $\dfrac{\text{stockholders' equity} - \text{preferred stock}}{\text{common stock outstanding}}$
per share

$$= \frac{\$830}{105} = \$7.90$$

g. Earnings = $\dfrac{\text{net income}}{\text{common stock outstanding}} = \dfrac{\$1,647}{105} = \$15.69$
per share

h. Price-earnings ratio = $\dfrac{\text{market price per share}}{\text{earnings per share}} = \dfrac{\$140}{\$15.69} = 8.92$

i. Dividends = $\dfrac{\text{dividends}}{\text{common stock outstanding}} = \dfrac{\$620}{105} = \$5.90$
per share

j. Dividend payout = $\dfrac{\text{dividends per share}}{\text{earnings per share}} = \dfrac{\$5.90}{\$15.69} = .38$

k. Debt ratio = $\dfrac{\text{total debt}}{\text{total assets}} = \dfrac{\$315}{\$1,145} = .28$

31. Milich Corporation's common stock account for 19X3 and 19X2 revealed that common stock at $10 par value equaled $40,000. Relevant data follow:

	19X2	19X1
Dividends	$2,500	$4,000
Market price per share	18	23
Earnings per share	2.00	2.80

a. Compute:
   1. Dividends per share
   2. Dividend yield
   3. Dividend payout
b. What do the ratios reveal?

---

a.

Dividends per share = $\dfrac{\text{dividends}}{\text{common stock outstanding}}$

| | 19X2 | | 19X1 | |

$$\frac{\$2,500}{4,000} = \$.63 \qquad \frac{\$4,000}{4,000} = \$1$$

$$\text{Dividend yield} \quad = \quad \frac{\text{dividends per share}}{\text{market price per share}}$$

$$\frac{\$.63}{\$18} = .035 \qquad \frac{\$1}{\$23} = .043$$

$$\text{Dividend payout} \quad = \quad \frac{\text{dividends per share}}{\text{earnings per share}}$$

$$\frac{\$.63}{\$2.00} = .32 \qquad \frac{\$1.00}{\$2.80} = .36$$

b. All the dividend ratios declined over the year. Investors will be concerned.

Self-Test

1. Examining financial statement information to predict future price of stock and dividends is referred to as _____.
2. The ratio of fixed cost to total cost is termed _____.
3. If sales increased from $12 to $16, the percentage change is _____%.
4. Common size financial statements show _____ analysis.
5. In a common-size income statement, net sales is given the value of _____.
6. Your salary increased from $20,000 to $25,000 the next year. What was your percentage increase in salary?
7. In performing ratio analysis, which year should you use as the base?
8. What current asset is excluded from the numerator in determining the quick ratio?
9. The combination of the age of receivables and age of inventory is the _____.
10. _____ is a company's ability to meet long-term debt.
11. The ratio of debt to equity is termed _____.
12. How is the interest coverage ratio computed?
13. Unfunded past pension expense is an example of an _____ liability.
14. Profit margin is the ratio of _____ to _____.
15. Market price divided by earnings per share is the _____ ratio.
16. The dividend yield ratio equals _____.
17. A ratio is a _____ measure, which is a limitation.
18. What effect will poor financial position have on the price/earnings ratio?

19. Match the columns.

1.	Earnings per share	A.	Dividends per share/market price per share
2.	Net working capital	B.	Current assets/current liabilities
3.	Price/earnings ratio	C.	Net income/shares outstanding
4.	Dividend payout	D.	365 days/accounts receivable turnover
5.	Current ratio	E.	Current assets – current liabilities
6.	Inventory turnover	F.	Dividends per share/earnings per share
7.	Collection period	G.	Income before interest and taxes/interest
8.	Dividend yield	H.	Market price per share/earnings per share
9.	Book value per share	I.	Stockholders' equity /shares outstanding
10.	Interest coverage	J.	Cost of sales/average inventory
11.	Return on stockholders' equity	K.	Net income/average stockholders' equity

20. Jones Corporation's financial statements appear below.

Jones Corporation
Balance Sheet
December 31, 19X1

Assets
Current Assets

Cash	$100,000	
Marketable securities	200,000	
Inventory	300,000	
Total current assets		$600,000

Noncurrent assets

Plant assets	500,000

Total assets	$1,100,000

Liabilities and Stockholders' Equity

Current liabilities	$200,000	
Long-term liabilities	100,000	
Total liabilities		$300,000

Stockholders' Equity
Common stock, $1 par value,
   100,000 shares $100,000
Premium on common stock   500,000
Retained earnings   200,000

    Total stockholders' equity   800,000

Total liabilities and stockholders' equity $1,100,000

Jones Corporation
Income Statement
Year Ended December 31, 19X1

Net sales $10,000,000
Cost of goods sold   6,000,000
   Gross profit $ 4,000,000
Operating expenses   1,000,000
Income before taxes $ 3,000,000
Income taxes (50% rate)   1,500,000
Net income $ 1,500,000

    Additional information available is a market price of $150 per share
of stock and total dividends of $600,000 for 19X1, and $250,000 of inventory as of December 31, 19X0. Compute the following ratios:

    a. Current ratio
    b. Quick ratio
    c. Inventory turnover
    d. Age of inventory
    e. Stockholders' equity to total liabilities
    f. Plant assets to long-term liabilities
    g. Operating expenses to net sales
    h. Earnings per share
    i. Price/earnings ratio
    j. Dividends per share
    k. Dividend payout

Self-Test Answers

  1. fundamental analysis
  2. operating leverage
  3. 33.3%
  4. vertical
  5. 100
  6. 25%
  7. the year most typical of business activity

8. inventory
9. operating cycle
10. Solvency
11. financial leverage
12. income before interest and tax divided by interest
13. undervalued
14. net income, sales
15. price/earnings
16. dividends per share divided by market price per share
17. static
18. It will lower the ratio.
19.
 1. C
 2. E
 3. H
 4. F
 5. B
 6. J
 7. D
 8. A
 9. I
 10. G
 11. K
20.
 a. 3
 b. 1.5
 c. 21.82
 d. 16.7 days
 e. 2.67
 f. 5
 g. .1
 h. $15
 i. 10
 j. $6
 k. .4

TECHNICAL ANALYSIS 5

Objectives

When you complete this chapter, you will be able to:

- Describe technical analysis
- Use techniques to appraise and evaluate the general market
- Cite contrary opinion indicators for the stock market
- Utilize tools to select individual stocks
- Chart market and individual stock movements
- Enumerate the forms of the efficient market hypothesis
- Define random walk theory

Tools of Technical Analysis

Technical analysts believe the market can be predicted in terms of direction and magnitude. They study the stock market using various indicators including an evaluation of the economic variables within the marketplace. Stock prices of companies tend to move with the market because they react to various demand and supply forces. The technical analysts try to predict short-term price changes and then recommend the timing of a purchase and sale. They attempt to uncover a consistent pattern in prices or a relationship between stock price changes and other market data. Technical analysts also look at charts and graphs of internal market data including prices and volume.

Figure 5.1 reflects the movement in the price of a company's stock.

You should be familiar with some of the terms used in technical analysis:

- *Momentum*: the rate of change of a stock price or market index over a period of time.
- *Accumulation*: a price rise on a large volume of stock that is moving from "weak hands" to "strong hands."

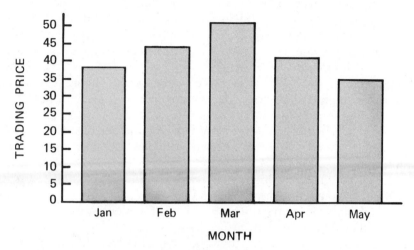

ACME MOTOR CO. STOCK

Figure 5.1   *Sample Company Stock Chart*

- *Distribution*: a price decline on a large volume of stock that is moving from "strong hands" to "weak hands."
- *Consolidation phases*: time periods during which price moves within a narrow band.
- *Resistance phases*: time periods during which prices move with difficulty.
- *Bellwether stocks*: stocks that accurately reflect the condition of the market (IBM, for example).

Technical analysts make certain assumptions, including the following:

- Chart patterns often repeat.
- Charts uncover shifts in demand and supply.
- Supply and demand are affected by logical and illogical variables.
- Supply and demand determine market price.
- Trend reversals result from changes in demand/supply relationships.
- Even though minor market fluctuations exist, the trend in stock prices lasts a long time.

The two primary tools of technical analysts are *key indicators* and *charting*.

Key Indicators

Key indicators of market and stock performance include trading volume, market breadth, Barron's Confidence Index, mutual fund cash position, short selling, odd-lot theory, and the Index of Bearish Sentiment.

Trading Volume

Trading volume trends indicate the health of the market. Price follows volume. For example, we expect to have increased price on increased volume.

Market volume of stocks is based on supply/demand relationships and points to market strength or weakness. Real and psychological factors influence stock buyers and sellers. A strong market exists when volume increases as prices rise. The market is weak when volume increases as prices decline.

If the supply of new stock offerings exceeds the demand, stock prices will decrease. If the demand exceeds the supply of new stock offerings, stock prices will increase. Supply/demand analysis is concerned more with the short term than with the long term.

Volume is closely related to stock price change. A bullish market exists when there is a new high on heavy trading volume. A new high with light volume, however, is viewed as a temporary situation. A new low with light volume is considered much better than one with high volume because fewer investors are involved. If there is high volume with the new low price, a very bearish situation may exist.

When price goes to a new high on increased volume, a potential reversal may occur where the current volume is less than the prior rally's volume. A rally with declining volume is questionable and may foreshadow a reversal in price. A bullish indicator exists when prices increase after a long decline and then reach a level equal to or greater than the preceding trough. It is a bullish indicator when volume on the secondary trough is less than the first one. When price declines on heavy volume, a bearish indicator exists pointing to a reversal in trend.

A *selling climax* takes place when prices decrease for a long period at an increased rate coupled with increased volume. After the selling climax, prices are expected to go up, and the low at the point of climax is not expected to be violated for a long time. A selling climax often occurs at the end of a bear market.

When prices have been rising for several months, a low price increase coupled with high volume is a bearish sign.

An *upside/downside index* illustrates the difference between stock volume advancing and decreasing and is usually based on a 10-day or 30-day moving average. The index is helpful in predicting market turning points. A bull market continues only where buying pressures remain strong.

An *exhaustion move* is the last stage of a major rise in stock price. It occurs when trading volume and prices drop rapidly. It usually points to a trend reversal.

A "net volume" service for major listed stocks to institutional investors is put out by Muller & Co. When net volume increases, accumulation is occurring. When net volume decreases, distribution is taking place. When the net volume line increases or stays constant while the price drops, accumulation under weakness is occurring and a reversal is anticipated. On the other hand, a decrease or constant net volume during a price rise indicates distribution under strength and an impending reversal.

Market Breadth

Market breadth is the dispersion of a general price increase or decrease. It can be useful as an advance indicator of major stock price declines and advances. A market breadth analysis can be used to examine the prime turning points of the market based on the theory of stock market cycles. A *bull market* is a long period during which particular securities reach their peak slowly with the number of individual peaks increasing as market averages approach a turning point. A *bear market* exists when the prices of many stocks decrease significantly in a short time period. To predict market weakness, we look to see whether many stocks are decreasing in price while the averages increase. To predict the end of a bear market, we consider the magnitude of selling pressure.

A market breadth indicator measures the activity of a broader range of securities than does a market average such as the Dow Jones Industrial. The Dow Jones stocks may not be representative of the entire market because the average is weighted toward large companies. Thus, all stocks on an exchange may be analyzed in terms of advances and declines.

The Breadth Index computes on a daily basis the net advances or declining issues on the New York Stock Exchange. A strong market is one that shows net advances. The degree of strength is based on the spread between the number of advances and the number of declines. The Breadth Index is determined by dividing net advances (number of securities with price increases) or declines (number of securities with price decreases) in the stock market by the number of securities traded. Relevant data can be found in the *Wall Street Journal*.

Advances and declines usually move the same way as a popular market average. They may, however, move the opposite way at a market peak or bottom.

Breadth analysis emphasizes change rather than level. Once you have determined the Breadth Index, you should chart it against a market average such as the Dow Jones Industrial. Typically, they will move together. During a bull market, technical analysts must carefully watch an extended divergence of the two—for example, where the Breadth Index declines gradually to new lows while the Dow Jones reaches new highs. The Breadth Index for the current year may also be compared to that of a base year.

As an example, let's assume net declines are 35. Securities traded are 1,240. The index is –2.8 (–35/1,240). We can compare this figure to a base year or we can include it in a 150-day moving average. Now let's take the figures we obtained and compare them to the Dow Jones Industrial Average. When the Breadth Index and Dow Jones Industrial Average are going down, market weakness is indicated. Of course, when the Breadth Index is going up with the Dow Jones Industrial Average, market support exists.

A possible indicator of the end of a bull market exists when the Dow Jones Industrial Average is going up but the number of daily declines is greater than the number of daily advances on a recurring basis. This shows that conservative investors are buying blue chips but lack confidence in the market as a whole. An upturn in the market may be indicated when the Dow Jones Industrial Average is decreasing, but advances repeatedly lead declines.

Breadth analysis assumes that many stocks decrease in price for a short time during a bear market. By looking at market breadth movement, we can predict a selling spree. In the last phase of a bear market, the net advance-decline line drops by several thousand, Dow Jones Industrials decrease several percentage points, and volume of trading significantly increases.

We can also use market breadth to examine individual securities. Net volume (rises in price minus decrease in price) is determined.

Now let's assume General Motors trades 110,000 shares for the day, with 70,000 on the upside (rising in price), 30,000 on the downside (falling in price), and 10,000 showing no change. The net volume difference at day's end is 40,000 traded on upticks (rises in price). We have to examine any sign of divergence between the price trend and the net volume of General Motors. When a divergence takes place, we can expect a reversal of the price trend. When price decreases and net volume increases, we know that accumulation is occurring.

Table 5.1   **Market Diary**

	Monday
Issues traded	1,200
Advances	820
Declines	305
Unchanged	75
New highs	94
New lows	26

Barron's Confidence Index

Barron's Confidence Index analyzes the trading pattern of investors in bonds. You can use it to ascertain when to purchase and sell stocks. This index is based on the belief that bond traders are more knowledgeable than stock traders and identify trends sooner. If we know what bond traders are doing today, we can predict what stock traders will be doing next. Many believe that there is a lead time of several months between the Confidence Index and what happens with the stock market. The index is published weekly in *Barron's*. The index is computed as follows:

$$\frac{\text{Yield on Barron's 10 top-grade corporate bonds}}{\text{Yield on Dow Jones 40 bond average}}$$

If the Dow Jones yield is 13% while the *Barron's* yield is 12%, the Confidence Index is 92.3% (12%/13%).

The numerator will have a lower yield than the denominator because it consists of higher-quality bonds. With bonds, as with any investment, lower risk means a lower return. Hence, since top-grade bonds have lower yields than lower-grade bonds, the index will be below 100%. Normally, the trading range is between 80% and 95%. When bond investors are bullish, yield differences between the high-grade and low-grade bonds will be small; in these instances the index may be near 95%.

If things are bearish, bond market investors will want to hold top-quality issues. Some investors who continue to put their money in average or lower-quality bonds will want a high yield for the increased risk. The Confidence Index will now decline, since the denominator will be getting larger. If confidence is high, investors are apt to purchase lower-grade bonds. As a result, the yield on high-grade bonds will decrease while the yield on low-grade bonds will increase.

Mutual Fund Cash Position

The *purchasing pattern of mutual funds* is often an indicator of the purchasing potential of large institutional investors. The ratio of mutual fund cash and cash equivalents to total assets is provided monthly by the Investment Company Institute. Changes in the figures show institutional portfolio management thinking. The ratio usually hovers between 5% and 25%. When a mutual fund's cash position is 15% of assets or higher, analysts assume the fund represents significant purchasing power that may indicate a market upturn. The stronger the cash position of the fund, the more bullish the general market outlook. When this cash is invested in the market, stock prices will increase. A low cash balance is a bearish sign.

Short Selling

Short selling occurs when investors believe stock prices will drop (see Chapter 2). Technical analysts look at the number of shares sold short. They also look at the ratio of latest reported short interest position for the month by the daily average volume for the month. (Short interest means the number of stocks sold short in the market at any given time). A high ratio is bullish and a low ratio is bearish. In the past, the ratio for all stocks on the New York Stock Exchange has hovered between 1.0 and 1.75. A short-interest ratio of 2.0 or greater would indicate a market low.

Looking at short sales is often called a *contrary opinion rule.* Some analysts believe that an increase in the number of short sellers indicates a bullish market. It is believed that short sellers get emotional and overreact. Also, the short seller will later purchase the short-sold stock. Increased short sales and increased market activity will create additional market supply. Then, when the market goes down, the short sellers will buy back their shares, and this will produce increased market demand.

Some analysts believe, however, that increased short selling reflects a downward and technically weak market that results from investors' pessimism. The short seller, in fact, expects a downward market.

The amount of short interest on the New York Stock Exchange and American Stock Exchange is published in the *Wall Street Journal* and *Barron's.* By monitoring short interest, you can foresee future market demand and determine whether the current market is optimistic or pessimistic. A very substantial short interest in a stock should make you question the value of the security. Short-interest information does have two limitations, however: (1) some studies have shown that short interest follows the same pattern as market price changes; and (2) data are sometimes not available until two weeks after the short sale occurs.

You should also examine odd-lot short sales. Many odd-lotters are unin-formed. An odd-lotter short sale ratio of around .5% indicates optimism; a ratio of 3.0 or more reflects pessimism.

Specialists do make markets in various securities listed on the organized exchanges, however, and they are considered "intelligent money." Watch the ratio of specialists' short sales to the total number of short sales on an ex-change. For example, if specialists sell 100,000 shares short in a week and the total number of short sales is 400,000, the specialists' sales constitute 25% of all short sales. Specialists' short sales are a bullish indicator. These specialists keep a book of limit orders on their securities, so they are knowledgeable as to market activity at a particular time. However, if most of their short sales are covered, this is a bullish sign. A normal ratio is approx-imately 55%. A ratio of 65% or more is a bearish indicator. A ratio less than 40% is bullish.

Odd-Lot Theory

Odd-lot trading (see Chapter 2) reflects popular opinion. The odd-lot theory rests on the rule of contrary opinion. In other words, you will determine what losers are doing and then you will do the opposite. Theoretically, knowledgeable investors should sell when the small traders are buying and buy when they are selling. Odd-lot trading data are published in the *Wall Street Journal* and *Barron's*. Volume is usually expressed in number or shares rather than dollars. Some technical analysts use the SEC Statistical Bulletin, however, in which volume is given in dollars.

An odd-lot index is a ratio of odd-lot purchases to odd-lot sales. This ratio usually stands between .40 and 1.60. Some investors look at the ratio of odd-lot short sales to total odd-lot sales, and the ratio of total odd-lot volume (buys and sells) to round-lot volume on the New York Stock Exchange. These figures serve to substantiate the conclusions they reached by analyzing the ratio of odd-lot selling volume to odd-lot buying volume.

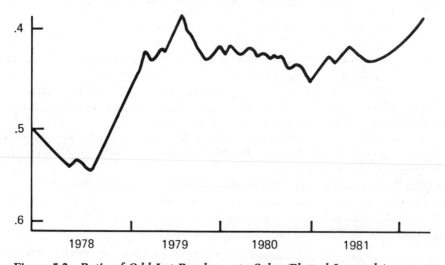

Figure 5.2   *Ratio of Odd Lot Purchases to Sales (Plotted Inversely)*

According to odd-lot theory, the small trader is right most of the time but misses key market turns. For example, odd-lot traders correctly start selling off part of their portfolios in an up market trend, but as the market continues to rise, the small traders try to make a killing by becoming significant net buyers. This precedes a market fall. In a similar vein, it is assumed that odd-lotters will start selling off strong prior to a bottoming of a bear market. When odd-lot volume rises in an increasing stock market, most analysts assume the market is about to turn around.

Stock market research does not fully support the odd-lot theory.

Index of Bearish Sentiment

Investors Intelligence has formulated an *Index of Bearish Sentiment* based on a reversal of the recommendations of investment advisory services. This index operates according to the contrary opinion rule: whatever the investment advisory service recommends, you should do the opposite. Investors Intelligence believes that when 42% or more of the advisory services are bearish, the market in fact will go up. On the other hand, when 17% or fewer of the services are bearish, the market will go down.

The Index of Bearish Sentiment is the ratio of bearish services to the total number of services giving an opinion. A movement toward 10% means the Dow Jones Industrial Average is about to go from bullish to bearish. When the Index approaches 60%, the Dow Jones Industrial Average is about to go from bearish to bullish. The reasoning of Investors Intelligence is that the advisory services are trend followers rather than anticipators. Therefore, the services' least bearish reports mean the market will drop, and their most bearish reports mean the market will increase.

Puts and Calls

A put is the right to sell a stock at a fixed price by a specified date. A call is the right to buy a stock at a fixed price by a certain date. Puts and calls are discussed in detail in Chapter 9.

Option trading activity may help you predict market trends. The put-call ratio equals put volume divided by call volume. The ratio increases due to more put activity from pessimism around market bottom. The ratio decreases due to more call activity from investor optimism around the market peak.

The option buy (initial option transaction establishing a long position) call percentage looks at open buy call transactions to total call volume. Investor optimism is reflected in a high ratio while trader caution is indicated in a low ratio.

Charting

You can use charts to evaluate market conditions and the price behavior of individual securities. Standard and Poor's *Trendline* gives charting information on many securities. In order to interpret charts you must be able to analyze formations and spot buy and sell indicators. Different analysts looking at the same chart pattern may come up with different interpretations. The three basic types of charts are: (1) line, (2) bar, and (3) point-and-figure.

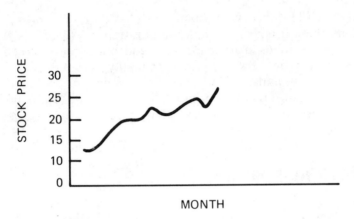

Figure 5.3   Line Chart

On line charts and bar charts, the vertical line shows price and the horizontal line shows time. On a line chart, ending prices are connected by straight lines. On a bar chart, vertical lines appear at each time period, and the top and bottom of each bar shows the high and low prices. A horizontal line across the bar marks the ending price.

Point-and-figure charts show emerging price patterns in the market in general or for specific stocks. Usually only the ending prices are charted. A rise in price is denoted by an X while a decrease is shown as an O. The chart may cover one year or less for active stocks or several years for nonactive ones.

In point-and-figure charts, there is a vertical price scale. Plots on the chart are made when a price changes by a predetermined amount. *Significant* price changes and their reversal are depicted. What is significant is up to the individual technical analyst. The analyst can use either ending prices or interday prices, depending on time constraints. The usual predetermined figures are 1 or 2 points for medium-priced stocks, 3 or 5 points for high-priced stocks, and ½ point for low-priced stocks. Most charts contain specific volume information.

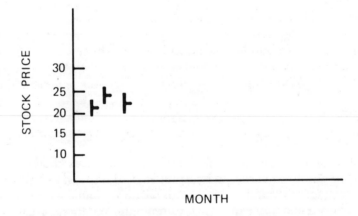

Figure 5.4   Bar Chart

Analysts should plot prices representing a trend in a single column, moving to the next column only when the trend is reversed. They will usually round a price to the nearest dollar and start by plotting a beginning rounded price. Nothing new appears on the chart if the rounded price does not change. If a different rounded price occurs, the analysts plot it. If new prices continue in the same direction, they will appear in the same column. A new column begins when there is a reversal.

Point-and-figure charts provide data about resistance levels (points). Breakouts from resistance levels indicate market direction. The longer the sideways movement before a break, the more the stock can increase in price.

You can use these charts to determine whether the market is in a major up- turn or downturn and whether the trend will reverse. You can also see what price may be accomplished by a given stock or market average. Further, these charts can help you predict the magnitude of a price swing.

Figure 5.5 is an illustrative point-and-figure chart. Notice there is no time dimension. A column of X's shows an upward price trend while a column of O's reveals a downward price trend.

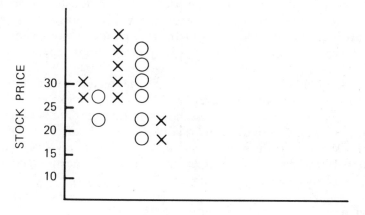

Figure 5.5   *Point-and-Figure Chart*

Moving Average

You can use *moving averages* to evaluate intermediate and long-term stock movements. (Moving averages are sometimes used for speculation in commodity futures.) By examining the movement of present prices compared to the long- term moving average of prices, you can foresee a reversal in a major uptrend in price of a particular security or the general market. A moving average shows the underlying direction and magnitude of change of very volatile numbers. It is determined by averaging a portion of the series and then adding the follow- ing number to the numbers already averaged, omitting the first number, and obtaining a new average.

Most analysts employ a 200-day moving average of daily ending prices. They often graph the average on stock price charts so they can see directions. You should buy when the 200-day average line becomes constant or rises after a decline and when the daily price of stock moves up above the average line.

Table 5.2   **Moving Average**

Day	Index	Three-Day Moving Total	Three-Day Moving Average
1	121		
2	130		
3	106	357 (Days 1–3)	119 (357/3)
4	112	348 (Days 2–4)	116 (348/3)

A buy is also indicated when stock price rises above the 200-day line, then goes down toward it but not through it, and then goes up again. You should sell when the average line becomes constant or slides down after a rise and when the daily stock price goes down through the average line. A sell is also indicated when stock price is below the average line, then rises toward it, but instead of going through it the price slips down again.

Relative Strength Analysis

Evaluating *relative strength* helps you predict individual stock prices. We get relative strength by computing a ratio of a monthly average stock price to a monthly average market index or industry group index. Another method is to compute the ratios of specific industry group price indexes to the total market index.

If a stock or industry group outperforms the market as a whole, most analysts view that stock positively since they feel that strong stocks and groups will become even stronger. Other analysts, however, differentiate between relative strength in a contracting market and relative strength in an expanding market. When a stock outperforms a major stock average in an advance, it may soon turn around. But when the stock outperforms the rest of the market in a decline, that stock will usually remain strong.

Support and Resistance Levels

A *support level* is the lower end of a trading range; a *resistance level* is the upper end. Support may occur when a stock goes to a lower level of trading,

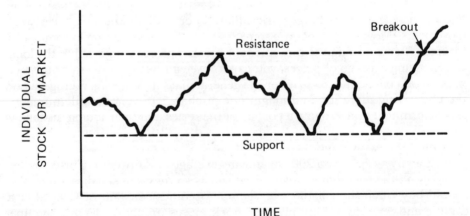

Figure 5.6   *Support and Resistance*

because new investors may now want to purchase it. If so, new demand will occur in the market. Resistance may take place when a security goes to the high side of the normal trading range. Investors who purchased on an earlier high may view this as a chance to sell the stocks at a profit. When market price goes above a resistance point or below a support point (in a "breakout") investors assume the stock is trading in a new range and that higher or lower trading values are imminent.

Dow Theory

The *Dow Theory* is the oldest and most widely used technique of technical analysis. It applies to individual stocks *and* to the overall market. It is based on the movements of the Dow Jones Industrial Average and the Dow Jones Transportation Average. Stock market direction must be confirmed by both averages. In Dow Theory, the price trend in the overall market is vital, since it is supposed to indicate the termination of both bull and bear markets. One limitation of this theory is that it is an *after* measure having no forecasting ability. It does not predict when a reversal will take place but merely confirms that the reversal has occurred.

The market is assumed to have three movements at the same time:

1. A *primary* trend can be either bullish or bearish and usually lasts 28 to 33 months.
2. A *secondary* trend runs counter to the primary movement and usually lasts three weeks to three months.
3. *Day-to-day* variability makes up the first two movements of the market.

Secondary movements and daily fluctuations are important because they reflect a long-term primary market trend.

According to the Dow Theory, a major primary increase in market averages co-exists with intermediate secondary downward reactions, eliminating a material amount of the previous rise. At the conclusion of each reaction, there is a price recovery that falls short of the prior high. If after an unsuccessful recovery, a downward reaction goes below the low point of the last prior reaction, the indication is that the market is in a primary downturn.

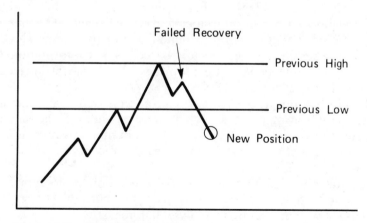

Figure 5.7 *Dow Theory Chart*

Here is the rationale of the Dow Theory: the market is up when the cyclical movements of the market averages increase over time and the successive market lows get higher; the market is down when the successive highs and successive lows in the stock market are lower than the previous highs and lows.

Many Dow theorists believe the action of the Dow Jones Transportation Average must confirm the action of the Dow Jones Industrial Average before a true bull or bear market signal is posted. Others believe the use of the Transportation Average in this manner has lost much of its validity, since these two averages will not usually follow the same pattern.

Efficient Markets and Random Walk

An *efficient market* is one in which a stock's price is the same as its investment value. In an efficient market, all data are completely and immediately reflected in price. Price changes in an efficient market are about equally likely to be positive or negative. The efficient market hypothesis applies most directly to large companies trading on the major securities exchanges. The various forms of the efficient stock market are weak, semi-strong, and strong.

In the *weak form*, there is no relationship between previous and future security prices. The two prices are independent over time. The informational value of historical information is already reflected in current prices. Thus, studying past stock prices is useless. In other words, the overall value of technical analysis is questionable.

The *semi-strong form* holds that stock prices adjust immediately to new data, and so action subsequent to a known event results in random results. All public information is reflected in a stock's value, and hence fundamental analysis cannot be used to ascertain if a stock is over- or undervalued. Investors quickly take information into account and can also see that changes in accounting methods have no economic meaning.

In the *strong form*, stock prices reflect *all* information—public and private (insider). Here we have a perfect market. The assumption is that no group of investors has monopolistic access to information. Assuming this, no group can earn superior risk-adjusted returns.

Random walk theorists believe that stock prices behave in a random and unpredictable fashion because the stock market is efficient. The market price of a company's stock goes randomly around real (intrinsic) value. However, the intrinsic value does change periodically based on new information. Current security prices are independent of prior prices. Thus, historical prices are not a reliable predictor of future prices.

According to random walk theory, financial data significant enough to affect future value is available to knowledgeable investors. Thus, the new data affecting stock price are immediately reflected in market value. At any given time, the price of a stock is the optimum estimate of its value including all available information.

Random walk theorists do not reject the prediction of stock prices based on accurate forecasting of corporate earnings and dividends. They do, however, reject the use of past market price analysis in forecasting future market price.

Review

1. What is technical analysis?

   _____

   Technical analysis is the study and interpretation of economic forces
   in the marketplace. By studying market factors such as prices and
   volume, the analyst can predict the future direction of the market.

2. (T,F) Technical analysis involves a detailed study of financial statement
   information.

   _____

   False. Technical analysis is an examination of the market. *Fundamental* analysis is based on an examination of financial statements.

3. (T,F) The technical analyst does not recommend the timing of a buy.

   _____

   False

4. The technical analyst believes that in a bearish market stock prices will
   a.   remain basically the same
   b.   rise
   c.   fall
   d.   fluctuate wildly

   _____

   c

5. The rate of change of a market index is called _____.

   _____

   momentum

6. A price rise on large volume is called _____.

   _____

   accumulation

7. _____ phases are periods during which prices move with
   difficulty.

   _____

   Resistance

8. _____ stocks accurately depict the present market state.

   _____

   Bellwether

9. _____ usually follows volume.

   _____

Price

10. When the number of highs is greater than the number of lows, the market is technically _____.

_____

strong

11. What is indicated when there is a sharp reduction in prices on high volume?

_____

market weakness

12. The market is _____ when there are excessive new offerings compared to demand.

_____

bearish

13. Explain the upside-downside index.

_____

This index helps the investor predict market turning points. It illustrates the differences between volume of stocks increasing and decreasing. It is usually based on a 10-day or 30-day moving average.

14. What is a selling climax?

_____

A selling climax occurs when prices fall for a long time at an increased rate coupled with increased volume.

15. What is an exhaustion move?

_____

The exhaustion move is at the last stage of a major rise in security prices. It takes place when trading volume and prices decrease sharply. Exhaustion moves generally reflect a trend reversal.

16. According to the "net volume" approach, what is indicated when there is a decrease in or constant net volume during a price rise?

_____

This indicates distribution under strength and an impending reversal.

17. What is the purpose of market breadth analysis?

_____

It studies the dispersion of general price increases and decreases. Market breadth serves as an advance indicator of major stock price changes.

18. An assumption of the _____ method is that many stocks reach their peaks and fall before the top of a bull market.

_____

   breadth of market

19. How is the breadth index computed?

_____

   by dividing the net advances or net declines in the market by the number of securities traded

20. What is the breadth index if net advances on the New York Stock Exchange are 27, and 1,250 securities are traded?

_____

   $$\frac{27}{1,250} = 2.16\%$$

21. Does a breadth index of 6% point to a bearish or bullish market?

_____

   The breadth index by itself does not reveal much. The index must be related to something.

22. What is indicated when the breadth index goes to new lows while the Dow Jones Industrial reaches new highs?

_____

   The inconsistency between the two indexes means that an increasing number of issues are turning down while the blue chips are going up.

23. _____ may be occurring when price falls and net volume increases.

_____

   Accumulation

24. Barron's Confidence Index assumes that _____ traders are more proficient than _____ traders.

_____

   bond, stock

25. Yields on _____ bonds are reflected in Barron's Confidence Index. It is a ratio of the yields of _____ grade bonds to _____ grade bonds.

_____

   corporate, high, low

26. If bond investors are positive about economic conditions, the Confidence

Index is relatively _____ and the yield differential between high-grade and low-grade bonds is _____.

high, small

27. In bearish times, the Confidence Index will _____.

decline

28. In evaluating mutual fund cash position, what ratio is examined?

cash plus cash equivalents to total assets

29. The lower the cash holdings of mutual funds the more _____ the market outlook.

bearish

30. (T,F) Analysis of short sales is based on the contrary opinion theory.

True

31. It is _____ when short sellers are pessimistic about the market.

bullish

32. A low short interest ratio is _____.

bearish

33. A _____ ratio of specialist short sales to exchange short sales is bearish.

high

34. (T,F) Odd-lot trading reflects popular opinion.

True

35. (T,F) Odd-lot trading is based on the contrary opinion theory.

True

36. **(T,F)** Technical analysts sell their stock when the odd-lot volume is high.

> True. They argue that little investors do the correct thing at the in-
> correct time. When small traders are buying, technical analysts sell.

37. How are some odd-lot ratios determined?

> odd-lot purchases to odd-lot sales; odd-lot short sales to total odd-lot
> sales; total odd-lot volume (buys and sells) to round-lot volume

38. If odd-lot buys begin to exceed odd-lot sales to great extent, this points
to the possible final stages of a _____.

> bull market

39. When almost all investment advisory services are bearish, we should be
_____.

> bullish

40. How is the put-call ratio determined?

> put volume divided by call volume

41. The ratio will _____ when there is greater call activity from
investor optimism around market peak.

> decline

42. In line and bar charts, the vertical axis shows _____ and the
horizontal axis shows _____.

> price, time

43. A bar chart plots all of the following except
   a. ending price
   b. beginning price
   c. shares sold short
   d. volume

> c

44. A point-and-figure chart has no _____ scale. It typically only
charts _____ prices.

time, ending

45. A significant change in a _____ stock is usually 1 or 2 points.

_____

medium-priced

46. In a point-and-figure chart, an increase in price is indicated by a(n) _____ while a decrease in price is depicted by a(n) _____.

_____

X, O

47. What does a moving average reveal?

_____

the underlying direction and magnitude of change in very volatile numbers

48. Based on the following, determine a three-day moving average.

Day	Index
1	112
2	123
3	108
4	114

Day	Index	Three-Day Moving Total	Three-Day Moving Average
1	112		
2	123		
3	108	343 (Days 1–3)	114.3 (343/3)
4	114	345 (Days 2–4)	115 (345/3)

49. According to moving average theory, investors should _____ stock when the average line becomes constant or _____ after a decline and the daily stock price goes above the average line.

_____

buy, rises

50. What are the implications of a common stock's price declining toward its 200-day average, turning up briefly, and then declining below it?

_____

The moving average method considers the facts as a sell situation.

51. What ratio can be computed to determine relative strength?

_____

$$\frac{\text{Monthly average stock price}}{\text{Monthly average market index}}$$

52. What is meant by a support level?

A support level is the lower end of a stock's normal trading range. Support may arise every time a stock goes to a lower trading level, since investors who have not already purchased may now decide to do so. It is a sign of new demand entering the market.

53. A _____ level applies to the upper end of a trading range.

resistance

54. The basis of the Dow Theory lies in the movement of the _____ and _____.

Dow Jones Industrial Average, Dow Jones Transportation Average

55. The premise of the Dow Theory is that the most important factor is the _____ in the overall market.

price trend

56. (T,F) The Dow Theory is supposed to point to the end of a bull or bear market.

True

57. The three movements in the Dow Theory that occur simultaneously are?

primary, secondary, and day-to-day

58. (T,F) The secondary trend typically lasts more than one year.

False

59. (T,F) According to the Dow Theory, an increase in the primary trend with the secondary troughs being successively lower points to a bearish market.

True. Successively less cyclical troughs result in the primary trend going down in the future.

60. According to the Dow Theory, if a recovery does not exceed the prior high and a new low penetrates a prior low, what can you conclude?

There is an end to an upward pattern.

61. Assume the Dow Jones Industrial Average is rising but there are net declines in the market. What does this indicate?

It shows the market may be going down in the future. A lack of broad confidence in the market exists.

62. Label each of the following "intelligent money" or "contrary opinion."
  a. Barron's Confidence Index
  b. odd-lot position
  c. short sales by specialists
  d. investment advisory services
  e. short sale positions

  a. intelligent money
  b. contrary opinion
  c. intelligent money
  d. contrary opinion
  e. contrary opinion

63. What form of the efficient market hypothesis says that later changes in prices of stocks have nothing to do with earlier ones?

weak form

64. What does the semi-strong efficient market hypothesis suggest?

Public information is reflected in the price of a security; hence fundamental analysis cannot be used to ascertain whether a stock price is under- or overvalued.

65. What does the strong form of the efficient market hypothesis assume?

All public and private information is impounded in the value of a security.

66. Random walk assumes an _____ stock market.

efficient

67. **(T,F)** If the random walk theory is accepted, technical analysis is useless.

True. With random walk, the assumption is that the independence of successive price changes refutes technical analysis.

Self-Test

1. Technical analysis bases stock selection on
   a. financial ratio analysis
   b. study of price and volume movements
   c. random walk theory
   d. the efficient market hypothesis
2. What is accumulation?
3. Securities that reflect the present market state are referred to as _____ stocks.
4. What is indicated by a significant jump in price occurring on high volume?
5. A _____ market exists when security prices are at new highs on heavy trading.
6. _____ analysis is usually based on a 10-day or 30-day moving average basis.
7. What occurs when prices decrease for a long period at an increased rate with increased volume?
8. _____ analysis is used to appraise the prime market turning points based on stock market cycles.
9. How is the breadth index computed?
10. What do we call the ratio of the yield on corporate high-quality bonds to the yield on the Dow Jones 40 bond average?
11. Where is the mutual fund cash ratio cited?
12. How is the mutual fund cash ratio computed?
13. If short sellers are pessimistic about the market, this is a _____ sign.
14. According to the odd-lot volume approach, what would be indicated if the public is selling in the lower end of the stock market?
15. Where can you find information on odd-lot trading?
16. When investment advisory services are bullish, we should be _____.
17. How is the put-call ratio calculated?
18. What kind of chart is the following?

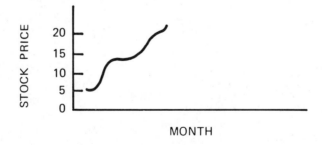

19. Describe how a bar chart looks.
20. With a point-and-figure chart, a decrease in price is indicated by a _____.

21. Using the data below compute a three-day moving average.

Day	Index
1	110
2	130
3	112
4	120

22. Most technical analysts use a _____-day moving average.

23. Relative strength is calculated by dividing the _____ by the _____.

24. A support level indicates _____ demand.

25. The upper end of a trading range is called the _____ level.

26. The Dow Theory concerns itself with movements in what two averages?

27. In the Dow Theory, what three movements occur at the same time?

28. What are some contrary opinion indicators?

29. What form of the efficient market hypothesis states that the value of a stock at any given time reflects all public and private information?

30. (T,F) Random walk rejects technical analysis.

31. Match the columns.

1.	Indicator of overall market	A.	Past prices do not predict future prices
2.	Efficient market hypothesis, strong form	B.	Past prices do predict future prices
3.	Random walk	C.	Advances and declines
4.	Technical analysis	D.	High level of normal trading range
5.	Contrary opinion	E.	Stock price includes all information
6.	Resistance level	F.	Investment service recommendations
7.	Support level	G.	Three major market movements
8.	Dow Theory	H.	Low level of normal trading range
9.	"Intelligent money" sign	I.	Specialist short sales
10.	"Small investor"	J.	Odd-lot

Self-Test Answers

1. b
2. price increases on high volume
3. bellwether
4. market strength
5. bullish

6. Upside/downside
7. selling climax
8. Breadth of market
9. net advances or net declines divided by the number of securities traded
10. Barron's Confidence Index
11. It is given monthly by the Investment Company Institute.
12. cash plus cash equivalents divided by total assets
13. bullish
14. This is a sign of technical strength and points to the advisability of purchasing stock.
15. New York Stock Exchange, SEC Statistical Bulletin
16. bearish
17. put volume divided by call volume
18. line chart
19. In a bar chart, the vertical axis is price and the horizontal axis is time. It depicts vertical lines for each time period. At the top and bottom of each bar are the highest and lowest prices for the period. A small horizontal line across each bar shows the closing price.
20. 0
21.

Day	Index	Three-Day Moving Total	Three-Day Moving Average
1	110		
2	130		
3	112	352 (Days 1–3)	117.3 (352/3)
4	120	362 (Days 2–4)	120.7 (362/3)

22. 200
23. monthly average stock price, monthly average market index
24. new
25. resistance
26. Dow Jones Industrial Average, Dow Jones Transportation Average
27. primary, secondary, and day-to-day
28. odd-lot position, investment advisory service, and short sales
29. strong form
30. True
31.   1. C
       2. E
       3. A
       4. B
       5. F
       6. D
       7. H
       8. G
       9. I
      10. J

COMMON STOCK INVESTMENTS

6

Objectives

When you complete this chapter, you will be able to:

- Describe common stock
- Understand stock quotations
- Identify the types of common stock
- State the characteristics that make common stock an attractive investment
- Describe two important trading techniques: margin trading and short selling

Securities Including Common Stock

The term *securities* covers a broad range of investment instruments, including common stocks, preferred stocks, bonds, and options. Two broad categories of securities are available to investors: *equity securities*, which represent ownership of a company, and *debt securities*, which represent a loan from the investor to a company or government. Each type of security has distinct characteristics as well as advantages and disadvantages that vary for every investor.

Common stock is an equity investment that represents the ownership of a corporation. It corresponds to the capital account for a sole proprietorship or capital contributed by each partner for a partnership. You should be familiar with the following common stock terms:

- *Shares*: A fractional ownership interest in a firm.
- *Par value*: The stated or face value of a stock; this figure exists primarily for legal purposes. Some stocks are issued with no par value.
- *Paid-in capital*: A difference between the par value and market value (what stockholders paid for common stock).
- *Retained earnings*: Net income accumulated over the years minus dividends paid out.
- *Book value*: An amount equal to the common equity (the sum of common stock, retained earnings, and paid-in capital) divided by the number of shares outstanding.
- *Liquidation value*: An estimate of the market value of the firm's assets, if sold at auction, minus liabilities and preferred stock outstanding.

The corporation's stockholders have certain rights and privileges including

- *Control of the firm*: The stockholders elect the firm's directors who in turn select officers to manage the business.
- *Preemptive rights*: This is the right to purchase new stock. A preemptive right entitles common stock holders to maintain their proportional ownership by being offered an opportunity to purchase, on a pro rata basis, any new stock being offered or any securities convertible into common stock.

Firms sometimes create special classes of common stock to meet specific needs and circumstances. If two classes of stock are offered, one is normally called "Class A" and the other "Class B." Holders of Class A stock might receive dividends before dividends can be paid on Class B. At the same time, however, Class B stockholders might have the exclusive right to vote.

You should understand the cash dividend and terms used in discussing it:

- *Cash dividends* are dividend payments made to the stockholder in cash.
- *The date of record* is the date on which the investor must be a registered shareholder to receive a dividend.
- *The payment date* is usually a few weeks after the date of record. It is the date on which the dividend checks will be mailed to holders of record.
- *The ex-dividend date* occurs four business days before the date of record. It determines who is eligible to receive the declared dividend.

Stock Quotations

The *Wall Street Journal* and other newspapers publish security price quotations. Price information for, say, the IBM stock traded on December 26, 1984, will be reported in the next day's paper in this form:

12-Month				Yld	P.E	Sales				Net
High	Low	Stock	Div	%	Ratio	100s	High	Low	Close	Chg.
128½	99	IBM	4.40	3.6	12	4183	124¼	123⅝	123¾	−½

The first two columns report the highest and lowest price at which the stock sold during the past fifty-two weeks. The cash dividend expected to be paid in 1984 is $4.40, based on the latest quarterly or semiannual declaration. The 3.6% *yld %* is the dividend yield, calculated by dividing the expected dividend ($4.40) by the closing share price (123¾) and rounding the answer to the nearest tenth of a percent. The next entry is the price/earnings ratio (often called the P/E multiple); this is the current market price divided by the previous year's per-share earnings. The daily volume follows the P/E ratio. For common stocks, sales are reported in lots of 100 shares. So 418,300 shares were traded on December 26, 1984. The High, Low, and Close columns indicate the highest, lowest, and last closing price at which the stock sold on December 26, 1984. The final column shows the net change between this day's closing price and the closing price on the preceding day. More details are included in "Explanatory Notes" following the newspaper's stock quotations.

Stock quotations for over-the-counter stocks are reported slightly differently. On December 27, 1984, the quotation for Apple appeared as follows:

Stock & Div.	Sales 100's	Bid	Asked	Net Chg.
AppleC	2999	27⅝	27¾	+⅛

This tells us that on December 27, 1984, Apple had 299,900 shares traded. You will remember that the bid price is the highest price for which the stock can be sold at the close of the day's trading, and the asked price is the lowest price for which the stock can be purchased. The last column on the right, Net Chg., shows the change in the asked price since the previous day. At the close of this day, one share of Apple stock could be sold for $27.625 and purchased for $27.75, which was 12½ cents (⅛) higher than the best purchase (asked) price on the preceding day.

The number of shares a company has outstanding affects market price per share. Usually, the greater the number of shares, the lower the price per share will be. This is true because a demand-supply relationship is at work. Furthermore, a thinly traded issue with a small number of shares outstanding tends to be more volatile in price.

Stock Dividends and Stock Splits

Quite often, a company will pay a dividend in stock instead of in cash. This is called a *stock dividend*; it is an issue of new shares expressed and distributed as a percentage of each shareholder's shares. For example, an investor who held 100 shares before a 10% stock dividend would hold 110 shares after.

A *stock split* is not a dividend. It is used whenever a company, believing the price of its stock is too high, wishes to enhance the stock's trading appeal and activity by lowering its market price. For example, in a two-for-one split, two new shares are exchanged for each old share, and the price is halved after the split.

Types of Common Stock

Common stocks fall into six different categories:

1. *Blue chip stocks* are common stocks of high quality that have a long record of earnings and dividend payments. These stocks are often viewed as long-term investment instruments; they have low risk and provide modest but dependable return. AT&T, Exxon, and DuPont are blue chip stocks.
2. *Growth stocks* have a long record of higher than average earnings and dividends. They generally grow faster than the economy as a whole and also faster than the industry of which they are a part. Examples include high-tech stocks in such fields as robotics.
3. *Income stocks* are characterized by a higher average and dividend payout ratios. These stocks are ideal for investors who desire high current income, rather than future capital gains, with little risk. Utility stocks such as AT&T and Consolidated Edison are income stocks.
4. *Cyclical stocks* are those whose earnings and prices move with the business cycle. Stocks of construction companies, building-materials firms, airlines, and the steel industry fall into this category.
5. *Defensive stocks* tend to remain relatively unaffected by downswings in the business cycles. In other words, they are recession-resistant. Stocks of utilities, soft drink companies, and consumer product firms are examples.
6. *Speculative stocks* generally lack a track record of high earnings and dividends; they have uncertain earnings, but have the chance to hit it big in the market. Many of the new issues such as cancer-related pharmaceutical stocks are a sheer gamble. These issues are ideal for investors who are willing to take risks in the hope for a big return.

You must be well informed and cautious when you invest in common stock. For example, the "penny stock market" consists of some over-the-counter stocks that are of high risk and low quality but possess high return possibility. They are sometimes referred to as cat-and-dog stocks. Some companies whose stocks have market prices in pennies per share may be on the brink of going out of business; others have just entered the market and are barely surviving. There is an exchange in Denver dedicated to penny stocks.

Stock prices may vary over the years. In 1981, for example, Chrysler stock was selling at about $5 a share. Those who sold their stock at that time incurred a huge loss. Now Chrysler stock is back up around $30 a share. The nuclear plant shutdown at Three Mile Island almost caused that public utility to go out of business. But it, too, has made a comeback. Penn Central would probably have gone bankrupt if it had not gotten rid of poor-return railroad assets and become a holding company with investments in different industries. Diversification greatly helped the company's stock performance.

Characteristics of Common Stock

The five characteristics that make common stock an attractive investment alternative can be summarized as follows:

1. Common stocks represent ownership of a company, as compared with fixed income securities such as bonds, which do not.

2. Common stocks provide an income potential not only in current income in the form of dividends but also in future capital gain.
3. Holders of common shares can receive part of the firm's earnings and lay claim to residual profits.
4. Common stock can be a good inflation hedge, if the total return from investment in common stock exceeds the rate of inflation.
5. Because a variety of stocks are available, the investor may choose from a broad spectrum of risk-return combinations from common stock investment.

A major disadvantage of common stock ownership is that common stock holders are the last to be paid in the event of corporate liquidation. Also, dividends omitted in a year do not have to be paid in a later year.

Margin Trading and Short Selling

Two common trading techniques are said to contribute to stock market efficiency. They are margin trading and short selling.

Margin trading is buying securities on credit. When an investor opens a margin account, he or she must sign a margin agreement similar to the agreement signed to obtain a bank loan. This document states the annual rate of interest, the method of computing that rate, and specific conditions under which interest rates can change. The Federal Reserve Board sets rules specifying the minimum percentage of the purchase price that a margin customer must pay in cash; this is known as a margin requirement. This requirement is now at least 50% of the current market value of the security. A 60% margin requirement means that 100 shares of a stock selling for $200 a share can be purchased by putting up, in cash, only 60% of the total purchase price—that is, $12,000—and borrowing the remaining $8,000 from the stockbroker, who then retains custody of the stock as collateral. (Some securities cannot be purchased on margin.)

This is a form of leverage that magnifies the gains and losses from a given percentage of price fluctuation in securities.

Another popular trading practice is *short selling*, a method some investors use in order to profit from a fall in stock price. In short selling, investors sell high, promising to buy back the stock later at what they hope will be a lower price. If the stock price falls, they make money. If it rises, they lose money (see Chapter 2).

A short seller has to set up a margin account with a stockbroker and comply with rules established by the federal government, the SEC, and the brokerage house. These requirements ensure that the investor will be able to buy back the stock if the price rises suddenly. Thus, the Federal Reserve requires a short seller to have in a margin account cash or securities worth at least 50% of the market value of the stock he or she wants to sell short. Another requirement is that a stock can be sold short only when the stock price has risen. An investor cannot sell short a listed stock that drops steadily from $50 to $30, for example. Stocks traded over the counter, on the other hand, can be sold short any time. Short sellers normally pay no interest charge. They must, however, keep the proceeds from the sale in their brokerage account. The firm invests that money in short-term securities and keeps the interest. The firm also gets its normal commission, which is usually from 1.5% to 2% on the sale and on the repurchase.

Because this trading practice can be extremely risky, investors often use certain short-selling strategies:

1. They sell short because they think the stock price is going to decline.
2. They sell short if they want to postpone making a gain and paying taxes on it from one year to the next. Let us suppose, for example, that the 100 shares of Apple you bought at $10 are now selling at $35 and you would like to sell the stock and take your profit. If you sell now, you will have to pay income taxes on the gain by next April 15. If you want to postpone the gain until the following year, you can tell your broker to short your Apple stock against the box. The broker will keep the stock certificate in a vault or box and sell it short. Because you own the stock and have sold it short, you have a hedge against increases or decreases in the price of Apple stock. If Apple rises to $50 a share by the time you sell it in January, you will have an additional $15-a-share gain on the stock you own but a $15-a-share loss on the stock you sell short. If, on the other hand, Apple falls back to $15, you will have no gain in the stock you originally purchased but a $25-a-share gain on the stock you sold short.
3. They sell short to protect themselves if they own the stock but for some reason cannot sell. If, for example, an investor buys stock through a payroll purchase plan at the end of each quarter but does not get the certificates until several weeks later, it may make sense for him to sell his shares short to lock in the gain.

Review

1. The term "securities" covers a broad range of investment instruments, including _____, _____, and _____.

   _____

   stocks, bonds, options

2. Two broad categories of securities are available to investors: _____ and _____.

   _____

   equity securities, debt securities

3. Equity interest is commonly thought of as
   a. mutual funds
   b. options
   c. bonds
   d. stocks

   _____

d

4. The value that represents the amount of shareholder's equity in a firm is called:
   a. book value
   b. par value
   c. market value
   d. liquidation value

a

5. The value that indicates what a firm would be worth on the auction block is
   a. book value
   b. market value
   c. liquidation value
   d. stated value

c

6. _____ is the right to purchase new stock.

Preemptive right

7. The date on which an investor must be a registered shareholder of the firm to be entitled to receive a dividend is called the
   a. purchase date
   b. declaration date
   c. ex-dividend date
   d. date of record

d

8. The difference between par value and market value is shown as _____.

paid-in capital (or capital surplus)

9. Dividend yield is found by dividing
   a. market price by the annual dividend
   b. earnings by the market price
   c. annual dividend by the market price
   d. dividends by the earnings

c

10. **(T,F)** The first two columns of the stock quotation, "High" and "Low," contain the highest and lowest price at which the stock sold during the past year.

    False

11. The "Yld %" in the quotation is the _____ yield, calculated by dividing the expected dividend by the _____ and rounding the number to the nearest _____ of a percent.

    dividend, closing share price, tenth

12. The bid price in the quotation for over-the-counter stocks is
    a. the lowest price
    b. the highest price
    c. the average of the lowest and the highest price
    d. none of the above

    b

13. If you held 100 shares of stock *before* a 10% stock dividend, how many shares would you own *after* the stock dividend?

    110

14. Why do firms use a stock split?

    It is used whenever a company, believing the price of its stock is too high, wishes to enhance the stock's trading appeal and activity by lowering its market price.

15. Stock in a corporation whose sales and earnings grow faster than the economy and the rest of the industry is called _____ stock.
    a. defensive
    b. income
    c. growth
    d. cyclical

    c

16. What type of stock has the greatest appeal to investors who want high current income with little risk?

    income stock

17.   Utilities, soft drink, and consumer product stocks are examples of
      _____.

      defensive stock

18.   What are blue chip stocks?

      stocks of high quality that have a long record of earnings and divi-
      dend payments

19.   The main advantage of common stock is its ability to hedge against:
      a.   interest rate risk
      b.   market risk
      c.   business risk
      d.   purchasing power risk

      d

20.   "Margin trading" means buying securities on _____.

      credit

21.   Selling short requires
      a.   no margin
      b.   no collateral
      c.   no delivery of securities
      d.   willingness to bear risk

      d

22.   Loss results from short selling when
      a.   interest rates fall
      b.   security prices fall
      c.   security prices rise
      d.   none of the above

      c

23.   A short sale against the box occurs when an investor
      a.   sells short shares that he or she actually owns
      b.   sells short on a minus tick
      c.   sells short an OTC stock that is listed on registered exchanges
      d.   none of the above

      a

24. **(T,F)** The short seller normally pays no interest charge.

_____

True

25. **(T,F)** You might consider selling short if you want to postpone making a gain and paying taxes on it from one year to the next.

_____

True

Self-Test

1. The ex-dividend date occurs _____ business days before the date of _____.
2. The liquidation value of a stock is an estimate of the market value of the firm's assets, if sold at _____, minus the liabilities and _____.
3. The price/earnings ratio, more often called the P/E _____, is the current market price divided by the _____.
4. Dividend yield is found by dividing the
   a. market price by the annual dividend
   b. earnings by the market price
   c. annual dividend by the market price
   d. expected dividend by the closing share price
5. The bid price is the _____ price the stock can be sold for, and the asked price is the _____ price the stock can be purchased for at the close of the day's trading.
6. **(T,F)** Stock dividend and cash dividend are the same.
7. What are cyclical stocks?
8. **(T,F)** Common stocks provide income potential not only in current income, that is dividend, but also in future capital gain.
9. **(T,F)** Margin trading is a form of leverage that magnifies the gains and losses from a given percentage of price fluctuation in securities.
10. **(T,F)** Investors might sell short when they think the stock price is going to rise.

Self-Test Answers

1. four, record
2. auction, preferred stock outstanding
3. multiple, per-share earnings
4. c
5. highest, lowest
6. False
7. stocks whose earnings and prices move with business cycles, such as stocks of construction firms, steel companies, and airlines
8. True
9. True
10. False

COMMON STOCK VALUATION

7

Objectives

When you complete this chapter, you will understand:

- The time value of the money concept—future value and present value
- Various valuation models of common stock
- How to use the P/E (price/earnings) ratio to forecast stock price

Time Value

The time value of money is a critical consideration in investment decisions, especially in evaluating stocks and bonds. For example, compound interest calculations are needed to appraise the future value of an investment. Discounting, or calculating present values, is inversely related to compounding. It is used to evaluate future cash flow from stocks and bonds.

Future Values: Compounding

A dollar in your hand today is worth more than the dollar you will receive tomorrow because of the interest it could earn if you put it in a bank account or some other investment. Compound interest occurs when interest earns interest. For the discussion of this and the subsequent time value concepts, let us define:

F_n = future value (the amount of money at the end of year n)
P = principal
i = annual interest rate
n = number of years

The future value of an investment if compounded annually at a rate of i for n years is

$$F_n = P(1 + i)^n = PT_1(i,n)$$

where $T_1(i,n)$ is the future value interest factor for one dollar (see Table 1 in Appendix C).

Future Value of an Annuity

An annuity is a series of equal payments, or receipts, for a specified number of periods. The future value of an annuity is a compound annuity that results from allowing these equal payments to grow. The future value of an annuity is computed as follows:

$$F = AT_2(i,n)$$

where A = the amount of an annuity and $T_2(i,n)$ = the future value interest factor for an n-year annuity compounded at i percent (see Table 2 in Appendix C).

Intrayear Compounding

Interest is often compounded more frequently than once a year. Some banks, for example, compound interest quarterly. To reflect this, adjustments are necessary in the previous formula. If interest is compounded m times a year, the general formula for calculating the future value becomes:

$$F_n = P(1 + \frac{i}{m})^{nm} = PT_1(\frac{i}{m}\ nm)$$

The formula reflects more frequent compounding (nm) at a lower interest rate per period ($i \div m$). The general rule is that the future value increases as m increases.

Annual Percentage Rate (APR)

Different types of investments use different compounding periods. For example, most bonds pay interest semiannually; some banks pay interest quarterly.

If you wish to compare investments with different compounding periods, you need to put them on a common basis. To do this, you will use the annual percentage rate (APR), or effective annual rate, which is computed as follows:

$$APR = (1 + \frac{r}{m})^m - 1.0$$

where r = the stated, nominal or quoted rate and *m* = the number of compounding periods per year.

Present Value: Discounting

Present value is the present worth of future sums of money. Calculating present values, or *discounting*, is the opposite of finding the compounded future value. Recall from the future value formula:

$$F_n = P(1 + i)^n$$

Therefore,

$$P = \frac{F_n}{(1 + i)^n} = F_n T_3(i,n)$$

where $T_3(i,n)$ represents the present value interest factor for one dollar (see Table 3 in Appendix C).

Present Value of an Annuity

Interest received from bonds, pension funds, and insurance obligations involves annuities. To compare these financial instruments, you need to know the present value of each of these annuities. The formula for finding the present value of an annuity is:

$$P = AT_4(i,n)$$

where A = the amount of an annuity and $T_4(i,n)$ = the value for the present value interest factor for a one dollar annuity at i percent for n years (see Table 4 in Appendix C).

Perpetuities

Annuities that go on forever are called *perpetuities*. An example of a perpetuity is preferred stock that yields a constant dollar dividend indefinitely. The present value of a perpetuity is found as follows:

$$\text{Present value of a perpetuity} = \frac{\text{receipts}}{\text{discount rate}} = \frac{A}{r}$$

Common Stock Valuation

The process of determining security value involves the present value of a securi-ty's expected future cash flows using the investor's required rate of return as the discount rate. Thus, the basic security valuation model can be defined mathematically as follows:

$$V = \sum_{t=0}^{\infty} \frac{C_t}{(1 + r)^t}$$

where V = the intrinsic value or present value of a security; C_t = expected future cash flows in period t; and r = the investor's required rate of return.

The value of a common stock is the present value of all future cash inflows that the investor expects to receive. The cash inflows expected are dividends and future stock price.

If an investor is holding a common stock for only one year, the value of the stock would be the present value of both the expected cash dividend to be received in one year (D_1) and the expected market price per share of the stock at year end (P_1). If r represents an investor's required rate of return, the value of the common stock today (P_0) would be:

$$P_0 = \frac{D_0}{(1 + r)^1} + \frac{P_1}{(1 + r)^1}$$

Present value and stock valuation calculations should be adjusted for in-herent risk in stock or cash flow projections. It is important to note that the market will often value stock differently over time than formulas might in-dicate, especially in capital gains calculations.

Since common stock has no maturity date and is usually held for more than one year, a more general, multiperiod model is needed. The general common stock valuation model is as follows:

$$P_0 = \sum_{t=0}^{\infty} \frac{D_t}{(1 + r)^t}$$

The model is based on the concept that a common stock is worth the pres-ent value of future dividends. However, future dividends may grow with three different patterns. as follows:

1. Zero growth
2. Constant growth
3. Nonconstant, or supernormal, growth

Zero Growth: If dividends are expected to remain unchanged, then the above model reduces to this formula:

$$P_0 = \frac{D_1}{r}$$

This is the case with a perpetuity. This model is most applicable to the valuation of preferred stocks or the common stocks of very mature companies such as big city electric utilities.

Constant Growth: If we assume that dividends grow at a constant rate of g every year (i.e., $D_t = D_o(1 + g)^t$), then the above model is simplified to give:

$$P_o = \frac{D_1}{(r - g)}$$

This is Gordon's growth model. This model is most applicable to the valuation of the common stocks of very large or broadly diversified companies.

Nonconstant, or Supernormal, Growth: Firms typically go through life cycles, during part of which they grow faster than the economy does and then fall sharply. When this happens, the value of the stock can be found as follows:

1. Compute the dividends during the period of supernormal growth and find their present value.
2. Find the price of the stock at the end of the supernormal growth period and compute its present value.
3. Add these two present value figures to find the value of the common stock P_o.

Expected Rate of Return on Common Stock

The investor's required rate of return is usually an offshoot to an acceptable level of risk.

The formula for computing the expected rate of return can easily be derived from the valuation models discussed previously.

The single-period return formula is:

$$r = \frac{D_1 + (P_1 - P_0)}{P_0}$$

In other words, r equals dividends plus capital gains divided by beginning price, which equals dividend yield plus capital gain yield.

This formula is, in effect, the same as the holding period return (HPR), when the current income is the dividend income, which was introduced in Chapter 3.

Many of these formulas are available on financial calculators such as the Hewlett Packard HP 12C.

The Price-Earnings Ratio: A Pragmatic Approach

The dividend valuation models discussed so far are best suited for those companies that are at the expansion or maturity stage of their life cycle. A more pragmatic approach to evaluating a common stock is to use the P/E ratio (or multiple). Many common stock analysts use this simple formula: Forecasted price at the end of year equals estimated EPS in year t times estimated P/E ratio.

Of course, for this method to be effective in forecasting the future value of a stock, earnings need to be correctly projected and the appropriate P/E multiple must be applied.

Forecasts of EPS

Forecasting EPS is not an easy task. Many security analysts use a simpler method—a sales forecast combined with an after-tax profit margin, as follows:

Estimated earnings in year t = estimated sales in year t × after-tax profit margin expected in year t

$$\text{Estimated EPS in year } t = \frac{\text{estimated earnings in year } t}{\text{number of common shares outstanding in year } t}$$

More sophisticated methods of forecasting sales and earnings, such as linear regression, are available and reserved for a more advanced text.

Determinants of the P/E Ratio

The determinants of the P/E multiple are numerous and complex. Empirical evidence seems to suggest the following:

- Historical growth rate in earnings
- Forecasted earnings
- Average dividend payout ratio
- Beta coefficient measuring the firm's systematic risk
- Instability of earnings
- Financial leverage
- Competitive position, management ability, economic conditions, and other variables

Review

1. _____ is a critical consideration in many investment decisions.

   _____

   Time value of money

2. $F_n = P(1 + i/m)^{nm}$ is a general formula used for _____.

   _____

   intrayear compounding

3. George Jackson placed $1,000 in a savings account earning 8% interest compounded annually. How much money will he have in his account at the end of four years?

    Substituting $P = \$1,000$, $i = .08$, and $n = 4$ into the formula and looking at Table 1 in Appendix C gives $F_4 = \$1,000(1 + .08)^4 = \$1,000(1.360) = \$1,360.00$.

4. In question 3, if the interest is compounded quarterly, how much will Jackson have?

    Now, $m = 4$. The formula looks as follows: $F = \$1,000(1 + .08/4)^{4.4} = \$1,000(1 + .02)^{16} = \$1,000(1.373) = \$1,373.00$.

5. The _____ is used to compare investments with different compounding periods.

    annual percentage rate (APR)

6. What is the APR if a bank offers 6% interest compounded quarterly?

    $APR = (1 + .06/4)^4 - 1.0 = (1.015)^4 - 1.0 = 1.0614 - 1.0 = .0614 = 6.14\%$

    If one bank offered 6% with quarterly compounding while another offered 6.14% with annual compounding, they would both be paying the same effective rate of interest.

7. The process of determining present value is often called _____ and is the inverse of the _____ process.

    discounting, compounding

8. A(n) _____ is a series of payments (or receipts) of a fixed amount for a specified number of periods.

    annuity

9. If an investor deposits $1,000 in a savings account at the end of each year, how much money will be in the account after six years if the annual interest rate is 8%?

    $1,000 (Table 2 value) = $1,000(7.336) = $7,336.00

10. You have an opportunity to receive $20,000 six years from now. If you can earn 10% on this investment, what is the most you should pay for this opportunity?

> Compute the present worth of the $20,000 you will receive six years from now at a 10% rate of discount. Use Table 3 value as follows:
>
> $20,000 (Table 3 value) = $20,000(.564) = $11,280.00
>
> This means that you should be indifferent to the choice between receiving $11,280 now or $20,000 six years from now since the amounts are time equivalent. In other words, you could invest $11,280 today at 10% and have $20,000 in six years.

11. Suppose you are to receive an annuity of $1,000 each year for the next three years at a 6% value of discount. What is the present worth of this annuity?

> Use Table 4 to compute the present value of an annuity as follows:
>
> $1,000 (Table 4 value) = $1,000(2.673) = $2,673

12. Which of the following is a perpetuity?
    a. preferred stock dividend
    b. common stock dividend
    c. interest income from bonds
    d. none of the above

> a

13. Assume that a preferred stock has an $80-per-year dividend payment and the discount rate is 10%. What is the present value of this perpetuity?

> $$\frac{\$80}{.1} = \$800$$

14. The valuation process involves finding _____ a security's expected future cash inflows using the investor's _____.

> present value, required rate of return

15. _____ model attempts to determine the value of a common stock when dividends are expected to grow at a constant rate.

> Gordon's growth

16. You are thinking about purchasing a stock at the beginning of the year. The dividend at year's end is expected to be $1.50, and the year-end market price is expected to be $40.00. You want to earn 15% on your investment. What is the value of the stock today?

You are looking for the present value of future cash inflows expected from this stock. Using Table 3 values gives:

$$\$1.50(.870) + \$40.00(.870) = \$1.31 + \$34.80 = \$36.11$$

17. Suppose that the stock you are considering pays the same dividend every year forever ($2.50). If you require a 10% return, what is the value of the stock?

This is a perpetuity; the value of the stock is $25: $2.5/.1 = $25.

18. Consider a common stock that paid a $3 dividend per share at the end of the last year and is expected to pay a cash dividend every year at a growth rate of 10%. Assume that the investor's required rate of return is 12%. What would be the value of the stock?

$$D_1 = D_0(1 + g) = \$3(1 + .1) = \$3.30$$

$$P_0 = \frac{D_1}{(r - g)} = \frac{\$3.30}{(.12 - .1)} = \$165$$

19. Consider a common stock whose dividends are expected to grow at a 24% rate for two years, after which the growth rate is expected to fall to 5%. The dividend paid last period was $2. The investor required a 12% return. What would be the value of the stock?

To find the value of this stock, we proceed as follows:
Step 1:

$D_0 = \$2.00$
$D_1 = \$2(1 + .24) = \$2(1.24) = \$2.48$
$D_2 = \$2(1 + .24)^2 = \$2(1.53) = \$3.08$
$D_3 = \$3.08(1 + .05) = \$3.08(1.05) = \$3.23$

The present value of dividends for the first two periods is $2.48 (Table 3 value, 12%, year 1) + $3.08 (Table 3 value, 12%, year 2) = $2.48 (.893) + $3.08(.797) = $2.21 + $2.45 = $4.66.
Step 2: Find P_2, as follows:

$$P_2 = \frac{D_3}{(r - g)} = \frac{\$3.23}{(.12 - .05)} = \$46.14$$

The present value of $46.14 is $46.14 (Table 3 value, 12%, year 2) = $46.14(.797) = $36.77.
Step 3:
Add the two figures obtained in steps 2 and 3 as follows:

$$P_0 = \$4.66 + \$36.77 = \$41.43$$

20. A stock sells for $50. The company is expected to pay a $3 cash dividend at the end of the year, and its market price at the end of the year is expected to be $55 a share. What is the expected rate of return on this stock investment?

$$\$3 + \frac{(\$55 - \$50)}{\$50} = \frac{\$3}{\$50} + \frac{\$5}{\$50} = 6\% + 10\% = 16\%$$

where 6% is the dividend yield and 10% is the capital gain yield.

21. Estimated earnings in year t are equal to estimated sales in year t times _____.

an after-tax profit margin expected in year t

22. The expected price per share of a stock at the end of year t is _____ times the estimated P/E ratio.

estimated earnings per share (EPS) in year t

23. List some of the variables that affect the P/E multiplier.

historical growth rate in earnings, forecasted EPS, average dividend payout ratio, beta coefficient, instability of earnings, financial leverage

24. The XYZ corporation had an EPS of $5. The EPS is expected to grow at 12%. The company's normal P/E ratio is estimated to be 7, which is used as the multiplier. What is the value of the stock?

Estimated EPS = $5(1 + .12) = $6. Therefore, the expected price of the stock is $6 × 7 = $42.

Self-Test

1. The formula for compound value is:
   a. $(1 + i)/P$
   b. $P(1 + i)^n$

    c. $P/(1 + i)$
    d. none of the above

2. **(T,F)** In the valuation formulas, r is the investor's required rate of return.

3. Since different types of investment use different compounding periods, it is important to distinguish the stated, or _____, rate and the _____ interest rate, often called the annual percentage rate (APR).

4. **(T,F)** An annuity is a stream of equal cash flows.

5. Your favorite uncle has offered you the choice of the following two options: He will give you $2,000 one year from now or $3,000 four years from now. Which would you choose if the discount rate (or your required rate of return) is 10%?

6. In the zero growth case, the calculation of P_0 requires the investor to estimate only
    a. a stream of dividends, r and g
    b. the return rate and the level of earnings
    c. D_0 and r
    d. D_1 and r

7. The equation $P_0 = D_1/(r - g)$ is used
    a. when the growth rate is supernormal
    b. in the zero growth case
    c. when the growth rate is constant
    d. in none of the above instances

8. **(T,F)** For the stock market, a P/E multiple that is high and increasing usually indicates investor optimism.

9. A firm's P/E ratio is assigned by
    a. stockholders at the annual meeting
    b. the market
    c. the NYSE
    d. the SEC

10. All of the following affect the value of a stock except
    a. future dividends
    b. future growth in dividends
    c. risk-free rate
    d. par value of stock

Self-Test Answers

1. b
2. True
3. nominal, effective
4. True
5. $2,000(.909) = $1,818 or $3,000(.683) = $2,049 (You would be wise to take $3,000 four years from now.)
6. a
7. c
8. True
9. b
10. d

FIXED INCOME SECURITIES

8

Objectives

When you complete this chapter, you will be able to:

- Describe the terms and the general features of *bonds*
- Understand bond quotations
- Identify the types of bonds
- Explain bond ratings
- Understand the yield curve
- State the advantages and disadvantages of bonds
- Discuss the method of valuing bonds
- State the characteristics of preferred stocks
- Discuss the valuation and rating system of preferred stocks

Bonds

A bond is a long-term debt obligation or a promise to pay by a corporation, government, or government agency. The bond issuer is obligated to pay you back your investment plus interest at a set date. Bonds, along with preferred stock, are called fixed-income securities.

Why Invest in Bonds?

Bonds provide investors with two kinds of income: interest income and capital gains. Interest income is current income. Capital gains are earned when market

127

interest rates fall. A basic trading rule in the bond market is that interest rates and bond prices move in opposite directions. If interest rates rise, bond prices fall and vice versa. So it is possible to purchase bonds at one price and, if interest rates fall, to sell them later at a higher price. Of course, it is quite possible to incur a capital loss. Bonds have long been considered suitable primarily for conservative investors such as retired people who rely on fixed income. Nevertheless, there is evidence that bonds have outperformed stocks on many occasions. Also, potential tax shields can be obtained with certain issues, such as municipal bonds.

Investors should be familiar with certain terms and features of bonds:

1. *Bond interest.* The interest on a bond is usually paid semiannually. The coupon rate determines the interest as the fixed return on the bond. The method of payment depends on whether the bond is a registered one or a coupon bond.
2. *Indenture.* The indenture, or deed of trust, is the legal agreement between the corporation and the bondholders. It contains the terms of the bond issue as well as any restrictive provisions placed on the firm. These *restrictive covenants* would include maintenance of (a) required levels of working capital, (b) a particular current ratio, and (c) a specified debt ratio.
3. *Trustee.* The trustee is the third party with whom the indenture is made. The trustee must see that the terms of the indenture are carried out.
4. *Yield.* The yield is the effective rate of return to the bondholder if the bond is held to maturity. It is different from the coupon interest rate.
5. *Call provision.* A call provision entitles the corporation to repurchase, or "call," the bond back from the holders at stated prices over specified periods.
6. *Sinking fund.* In a sinking fund, money is put aside periodically for the repayment of debt, thus reducing the total amount of debt outstanding. This particular provision may be included in the bond indenture to protect investors.

Types of Bonds

The many types of bonds include the following:

1. *Mortgage bonds* are secured by physical property.
2. *Debentures* are unsecured bonds. They are protected by the general credit of the issuing corporation. Credit ratings are very important for this type of bond. Federal, state, and municipal government issues are debentures. Subordinated debentures are junior issues ranking after other unsecured debt as a result of explicit provisions in the indenture. Finance companies have made extensive use of these types of bonds.
3. *Convertible bonds* are subordinated debentures that may be converted, at the option of the bondholder, into a specified amount of other securities (usually common stock) at a fixed price. The convertible feature is used as a sweetener.

4. *Income bonds* pay interest only if it is earned. They are often called reorganization bonds.
5. *Tax-exempt bonds* are usually state and municipal bonds where interest income is not subject to federal tax.
6. *Revenue bonds* are issued by municipalities and are serviced from the income generated by specific income-producing projects (e.g., highway tolls). Revenue bonds are a first lien on specific revenue streams, and are more secure in some instances than "general faith and credit"-type bonds.
7. *U.S. government securities* include bills, notes, and bonds. U.S. government notes have a maturity of one to seven years, whereas U.S. bonds have a maturity of seven to twenty-five years and can be purchased in denominations as low as $1,000. All these types of U.S. government securities are subject to federal income and capital gain taxes, but not to state and local income taxes. The government has moved from coupon-bearer bonds to registered bonds so that income now has to be reported to the Internal Revenue Service.
8. *Zero-coupon bonds* add the interest to the principal semiannually. Both the principal and the accumulated interest are paid at maturity. They are not fixed-income securities in the historical sense, because they provide no periodic income. The interest on the bond is paid at maturity. However, due to the 1984 Tax Reform Act, accrued interest, *though not received,* is taxable yearly as ordinary income. Table 8.1 shows some zero-coupon bonds.

Table 8.1 **Selected Zero-Coupon Bonds**

Firm Name	Maturity	Approximate Price
Allied Corporation	1987	70
Bank America	1991	45
Prudential Realty	1993	30

Yield to maturity is fairly constant for the same length investments, except for risk differences. Of course, one advantage of deep discount bonds is the lower entry price for smaller investors.

Bond Ratings

Bond ratings reflect the probability that a bond issue will go into default. They can influence investors' perception of risk, and they therefore have an impact on the interest rate. Bond investors tend to place more emphasis on independent analysis of quality than do common stock investors. Bond analysis and ratings are done by Standard and Poor's and Moody's, among others. Below is an actual listing of the designations used by these well-known independent agencies. Descriptions of ratings are summarized. For original versions of descriptions, see Moody's *Bond Record* and Standard and Poor's *Bond Guide.*

DESCRIPTION OF BOND RATINGS

Moody's	Standard and Poor's	Quality Indication
Aaa	AAA	Highest quality
Aa	AA	High quality
A	A	Upper medium grade
Baa	BBB	Medium grade
Ba	BB	Contains speculative elements
B	B	Outright speculative
Caa	CCC & CC	Default definitely possible
Ca	C	Default, only partial recovery likely
C	D	Default, little recovery likely

Bond investors pay careful attention to ratings since they can affect not only potential market behavior but relative yields as well. Specifically, the higher the rating the lower the yield of a bond, other things being equal. It should be noted that the ratings do change over time and the rating agencies have "credit watch lists" of various types. Buyer should be aware: Changes in creditworthiness can have dramatic impact on the current value of a bond—and on volatility of price.

Bond Quotations

To see how bond quotations are presented in the newspaper, let us look at the data for the IBM bond:

Bonds	Cur Yld	Vol	High	Low	Close	Net Chg
IBM 9⅜ 04	11.	169	84⅝	84	84	−1⅛

The numbers immediately following the company name give the bond coupon rate and maturity date. This particular bond carries a 9.375% interest rate and matures in the year 2004. The next column, Cur Yld, provides the current yield calculated by dividing the annual interest income (9⅜%) by the current market price of the bond (a closing price of 84). Thus the current yield for the IBM bond is 11%. This figure represents the effective, or real, rate of return on the current market price represented by the bond's interest earnings.

The Vol column shows the number of bonds traded on this day (169 bonds).

The market price of a bond is usually expressed as a percent of its par (face) value, which is customarily $1,000. *Corporate bonds* are quoted to the nearest *one-eighth* of a percent. The figure 84⅝ in the sample quotation indicates a price of $846.25, or 84⅝ of $1,000. Because U.S. government bonds are highly marketable and are bought and sold in keenly competitive markets, they are quoted in *thirty-seconds* or *sixty-fourths*. Moreover, decimals are used, rather than fractions, in quoting U.S. government bond prices. For example, a quotation of 106.17 for a Treasury bond indicates a price of $1,065.31. When a plus sign follows the quotation, the Treasury bond is being quoted in *sixty-fourths*. We must double the number following the decimal point and add one to determine the fraction of $10 represented in the quote. For example, a quote of 95.16+ indicates a price of $955.16.

Disadvantages of Bond Ownership

Investors should be aware that there are disadvantages to bond investment. One problem is the relatively large denominations, such as $1,000 an issue. Another is that interest income is fixed over the life term and is therefore vulnerable to inflation. Also, bond prices are sensitive to swings in market interest rates, which can cause substantial capital losses. Finally, the inactive secondary market limits investor liquidity (although certain segments of the bond market are quite active, especially in widely traded government issues).

The Yield Curve

We noted previously that interest rates and bond prices move in opposite directions. The investor who wishes to make a substantial profit in the bond market must have a good understanding of the turns and directions of interest rates. Although it is not easy to predict interest rates, it helps to consider the relationship between the level of interest rates and the maturity of the bond. The relationship between these two variables is called the *term structure of interest rates* and is captured in a *yield curve*. A yield curve depicts how yields respond to changes in maturity. It can shift upward, become flat, or even descend. Information about yield curves is useful in anticipating what interest rates should do in the future and in understanding how they can affect bond prices and comparative returns.

Bond Valuation

The valuation process for a bond requires knowledge about three basic elements: (1) the amount of the cash inflows to be received by the investor composed of the periodic interest receipts and the par value (face value) at maturity; (2) the maturity date of the debt obligation; and (3) the investor's required rate of return. Incidentally, the periodic interest receipts can be annual or semiannual. The value of a bond is simply the present worth of these cash inflows. Two versions of the bond valuation model are presented below:

1. If the interest payments are annual,

$$V = \sum_{t=1}^{n} \frac{I}{(1 + r)^t} + \frac{M}{(1 + r)^n}$$

$$= IT_4(r,n) + MT_3(r,n)$$

where I = interest payments each year = coupon interest rate × par value; M = the par value, or maturity value, typically $1,000; r = the investor's required rate of return on the bond; and n = the number of years to maturity. T_3 and T_4 are present value factors, which were discussed in Chapter 7.

2. If the interest payments are semiannual,

$$V = \frac{I}{2} T_4 \left(\frac{r}{2}, 2n\right) + MT_3 \left(\frac{r}{2}, 2n\right)$$

Note that the interest rate is halved as the number of periods doubles.

Rates of Return (Yields)

Bonds are evaluated on many different types of returns including current yield, yield to maturity, yield to call, and realized yield.

Current Yield: The current yield is the annual interest payment divided by the current price of the bond. This is reported in the *Wall Street Journal.*

Yield to Maturity: The yield to maturity is the real return an investor would receive from interest income plus capital gain, assuming the bond is held to maturity. The exact way of calculating this measure is a little complicated and not presented here. The approximate method is

$$\text{Yield} = \frac{I + (F - V)/n}{(F + V)/2}$$

where V = the market value of the bond and F = the face or par value.

Yield to call: If the bond can be called, the yield formulas above will have the call price in place of the par value.

Realized yield: Bond investors often trade in and out of a bond long before it matures. They obviously need a measure of return to evaluate the investment appeal of any bonds they intend to buy and sell. Realized yield is used for this purpose. This measure is simply a variation of yield to maturity, as only two variables are changed in the yield-to-maturity formula to provide this measure. Future price is used in place of par value, and the length of holding period is used in place of the number of years to maturity.

Preferred Stock

Preferred stock is in a way a hybrid of common stock and bonds. It represents an equity investment, but it has many of the characteristics associated with a bond issue:

1. It has a par value, normally $25 or $100.
2. The preferred dividend is normally fixed in amount and stated either as a percentage of par value or in dollars.
3. Most preferred stock is *cumulative*, which means that any unpaid preferred dividends must be paid before any dividends can be paid on the common stock.

4. Preferred stocks are riskier for investors than bonds because: (a) they come after bonds in the event of liquidation; and (b) bond interest is more likely to be paid in case of financial difficulty than are preferred dividends.
5. Because they are riskier than bonds, preferred stocks generally provide investors with a higher after-tax rate of return.
6. Preferred stock is particularly attractive to corporate investors because of the 85% dividend exclusion.
7. Preferred stock has no maturity date, but it is often *convertible* into common stock at the option of the preferred stockholders.

Valuation and Ratings of Preferred Stock

The key measure of return on preferred investment is the dividend yield:

$$\text{Dividend yield} = \frac{\text{annual stated dividend income}}{\text{preferred stock price}}$$

Standard and Poor's and Moody's have long rated the investment quality of preferred stocks. S & P uses basically the same rating system for both stocks and bonds, except that they do not give AAA to preferred shares. Moody's uses the following preferred stock rating system:

Grade	Description
aaa	Top quality
aa	High grade
a	Upper medium grade
baa	Lower medium grade
ba	Speculative
b	Little assurance of future dividends
caa	Arrears in dividend payments

Review

1. Bonds, along with _____, are called fixed-income securities.

_____

   preferred stock

2. Bond indenture
   a. contains the protective covenants
   b. states the bond's current rating
   c. states the yield to maturity of the bond
   d. all of the above

_____

   a

3. **(T,F)** The yield is the same as the coupon interest rate.

_____

False

4. A debenture is a(n) _____ bond.

_____

unsecured

5. **(T,F)** A mortgage bond is secured by a lien on real property.

_____

True

6. **(T,F)** The rating awarded to a specific issue of bonds tells much about the absolute probability of default.

_____

False

7. Name two well-known bond rating agencies.

_____

Moody's, Standard and Poor's

8. The highest rating that a bond can have is _____.

_____

AAA

9. Standard provisions in a restrictive covenant include maintenance of
   a. required levels of working capital
   b. a particular current ratio
   c. a specific debt/equity ratio
   d. all of the above

_____

d

10. In the bond quotations, the numbers immediately following the company name give the _____ and _____.

_____

bond coupon rate, maturity date

11. In bond quotations, the Cur Yld column provides _____, calculated by dividing the annual interest income by the _____ of a bond.

_____

the current yield, current market price

12. **(T,F)** One disadvantage of bond ownership is that the interest income is fixed over the life term and therefore is vulnerable to inflation.

_____

True

13. Bond prices and interest rates are _____ related.

_____

inversely

14. A bond's yield to maturity depends on
   a. the coupon rate
   b. the maturity of the bond
   c. the bond rating
   d. all of the above

_____

d

15. If the market price of a bond decreases,
   a. the coupon rate increases
   b. the yield to maturity decreases
   c. the yield to maturity increases
   d. a and b

_____

c

16. The widely accepted explanations of the shape of the yield curve are
   a. expectation theory
   b. liquidity theory
   c. market segmentation
   d. all of the above

_____

d

17. What three basic elements determine the value of a bond?

_____

the amount of cash inflows, the maturity date, and the investor's required rate of return

18. Bonds are evaluated on many different types of returns. What are they?

_____

current yield, yield to maturity, yield to call, and realized yield

19. Consider a bond maturing in ten years and having a coupon rate of 8%. The par value is $1,000. Investors consider 10% an appropriate required rate of return in view of the risk involved. Assume the interest payment is annual. What is the value of the bond?

The annual interest payment is $80 (8% × $1,000). Thus, the present value of the bond is

$80 (Table 4 value, 10%, 10 years) + $1,000 (Table 3 value, 10%, 10 year)
= $80(6.145) + $1,000(.386)
= $491.60 + $386.00 = $877.60

20. **(T,F)** Like common stock, preferred stock pays a dividend that varies with earnings.

False

Self-Test

1. The _____ is the third party involved in a bond indenture.
2. The rate of return on bonds is measured by _____, _____, _____, or _____.
3. **(T,F)** The coupon interest rate is different from the yield.
4. List the types of bonds.
5. What agencies rate bonds and preferred stocks?
6. In the bond quotations, what is the meaning of "IBM 9⅜ 04"?
7. The current yield is the annual interest divided by the _____ of the bond.
8. Bonds are subject to
   a. inflation risk
   b. default risk
   c. purchasing power risk
   d. all of the above
9. **(T,F)** The higher the interest rate, the lower the bond price.
10. Bond prices are sensitive to swings in _____.
11. Preferred stock represents a(n) _____ investment, but it has many of the characteristics associated with a(n) _____ issue.

Self-Test Answers

1. trustee
2. the current yield, yield to maturity, yield to call, realized yield
3. True
4. mortgage bonds, debentures, convertible bonds, income bonds, tax-exempt bonds, revenue bonds, U.S. government securities, zero-coupon bonds
5. Standard and Poor's and Moody's

6. This IBM bond carries a 9.375% interest rate and matures in the year 2004.
7. current market price
8. d
9. True
10. market interest rate
11. equity, bond

OPTIONS

Rights, Warrants, Calls and Puts

9

Objectives

When you complete this chapter, you will be able to:

- Distinguish between the different types of options
- Determine the value of an option and the rate of return on investment
- Understand opinion quotes
- Describe the advantages of receiving stock rights from a company already owned
- Explain the use of stock warrants in connection with debt issuances
- Enumerate the use of stock options by hedgers and speculators
- Define the investment merits of calls and puts
- Present the investment approaches of straddles and spreads
- Enumerate the functions of an option writer

What Are Options?

Options give you the right to purchase a security at a specified price for a stated period of time. Options possess their own inherent value and are traded in secondary markets. You may want to acquire an option so that you can take advantage of an expected rise in the price of the underlying stock. Option prices are directly related to the prices of the common stock they apply to. The types of options include rights, warrants, and calls and puts. Investing in options is *very risky* and requires specialized knowledge.

Stock Rights

In a stock rights offering, current stockholders have the first right to buy new shares and thus to maintain their present ownership interest. This is known as a *preemptive right*. Let's say, for example, that you own 3% of XYZ Company. If the company issues 5,000 additional shares, you may receive a stock rights offering—a chance to buy 3%, or 150 shares, of the new issue. This right enables you to purchase new common stock at a subscription price (sometimes called an exercise price) for a short time, usually no more than several weeks. This subscription price, or exercise price, is lower than the current market price of the stock.

If a company has, say, 2 million shares outstanding and wants to issue another 100,000 shares, each existing stockholder will receive one right per share owned. Thus, a stockholder needs 20 rights in order to buy one new share.

One advantage of the stock rights option is of course the lower exercise price. Another is that stockholders do not have to pay a brokerage fee when they buy the additional stock.

Stockholders who do not want to buy additional stock can sell their rights in the secondary market. (Of course, if a right is not used before the expiration date, it no longer has value.)

The value of a right depends on whether the stock is traded *rights-on* or *rights-off*. In a rights-on trade, the stock is traded with rights attached so the investor who purchases a share receives the attached stock right. In a rights-off or ex-rights trade, the stock and its rights are separate from each other and are traded in different markets. Regardless of the form of the rights, the value of a right equals

$$\frac{\text{Market price of current stock} - \text{subscription price of new stock}}{\text{Number of rights to purchase one share}}$$

Assume the current market price of stock is $30 a share. The new share has an exercise price of $26. An investor needs two rights to obtain one new share. The right equals:

$$\frac{\$30 - \$26}{2} = \frac{\$4}{2} = \$2$$

Provided the stock price holds at around $30 a share, the right has a value of $2.

Here is a quote for an assumed right:

12-MONTH		STOCK	SALES 100s	YIELD	WEEK'S	
High	Low				High	Low
47	22	XYZ Company	112	3.8	38⅛	36¼

Stock Warrants

A warrant is an option to purchase a certain number of shares at a stated price for a specified time period at a subscription price that is *higher* than the current market price. A warrant may or may not come in a one-to-one ratio with stock already owned. Unlike an option, a warrant is usually good for several years; some, in fact, have no maturity date.

Warrants are often given as sweeteners for a bond issue. This allows the firm to float the debt or issue the bond at a lower interest rate. Warrants included with a bond may also occur in a merger when the acquiring company offers cash plus warrants in exchange for the voting common stock of the acquired business. Generally, warrants are detachable from the bond, once it has been issued. Detachable warrants have their own market price. So even though warrants are exercised, the debt with which they were first issued still exists. Also stock warrants may be issued with preferred stock. Most warrants are traded on the American Stock Exchange, and some are traded on the New York Stock Exchange.

Warrants are not frequently issued and are not available for all securities. They pay no dividends and carry no voting privileges. The warrant enables the holder to take part *indirectly* in price appreciation of common stock and to obtain a capital gain. One warrant usually equals one share, but in some cases more than one warrant is needed to get one share.

Warrants can be bought from a broker. The price of a warrant is usually listed along with that of the common stock of the company. Brokerage fees for warrants are the same as those for stocks and depend on the market price of the security.

When the price per common share goes up, the holder of the warrant may either sell it (since the warrant also increases in value) or exercise the warrant and get the stock. Trading in warrants is speculative; there is potential for high return, but high risk exists because of the possibility of variability in return.

For accounting purposes, warrants are considered a common stock equivalent since their convertibility will increase the number of common shares outstanding. Thus, they dilute the earnings per share.

As we said earlier, when warrants are issued, the exercise price is greater .nan the market price. Assume a warrant of XYZ Company stock enables you to purchase one share at $25. If the stock increases past $25 before the expiration date, the warrant increases in value. If the stock goes below $25, the warrant loses its value.

The exercise price for a warrant is usually constant over the warrant's life. However, the price of some warants may rise as the expiration date approaches. Exercise price is adjusted for stock splits and large stock dividends.

The return on a warrant for a holding period of no more than one year equals:

$$\frac{\text{Selling price} - \text{acquisition price}}{\text{Acquisition price}}$$

Say that you sell a warrant at $21. That same warant cost you only $12. The return is:

$$\frac{\$21 - \$12}{\$12} = \frac{\$9}{\$12} = 75\%$$

The return on a warrant for a holding period in excess of one year equals:

$$\frac{\dfrac{\text{Selling price} - \text{acquisition price}}{\text{Years}}}{\text{Average investment}}$$

Let's say that there is a holding period of four years on the warrant you just sold for $21. The return is:

$$\frac{\dfrac{\$21 - \$12}{4}}{\dfrac{\$21 + \$12}{2}} = \frac{\$2.25}{\$16.5} = 13.6\%$$

Warrants are speculative because their value depends on the price of the common stock for which they can be exchanged. If stock prices fluctuate widely, the value of warrants will sharply vacillate.

The value of a warrant is greatest when the market price of the related stock is equal to or greater than the exercise price of the warrant. The value of a warrant thus equals:

(Market price of common stock – exercise price of warrant) × number of common stock shares bought for one warrant

For example, suppose that a warrant has an exercise price of $25. Two warrants equal one share. The market price of the stock is $30. The warrant has a value of:

($30 – $25) × .5 = $2.50

Usually the market value of a warrant is greater than its intrinsic value, or *premium*, because of the speculative nature of warrants. Typically, as the value of a warrant goes up, the premium goes down. Premium equals the market price of the warrant minus its intrinsic value. For example, if the warrant referred to above has a market price of $4.00, the premium is $1.50.

Assume that $100,000 in bonds are issued. There are therefore 100 bonds. Each bond has eight warrants attached. Each warrant permits the investor to purchase one share of stock at $12 until one year from the date of the bond. The warrant will have no value at the issue date if the stock is selling below $12. If the stock increases in value to $25 a share, the warrant will be worth about $13. The eight warrants will thus be worth approximately $104.

Assume XYZ common stock is $40 per share. One warrant can be used to buy one share at $34 in the next three years. The intrinsic (minimum) value per warrant is $6—($40 – $34) × 1. Because the warrant has three years left and can be used for speculation, it may be traded at an amount higher than $6. Assuming the warrant was selling at $8, it has a premium of $6. The premium is the $2 difference between warrant price and intrinsic value.

Even when the stock is selling for less than $34 a share, there might be a market value for the warrant because speculators may wish to buy it on the expectation of an attractive increase in common stock price in the future. For instance, if the common stock was at $30, the warrant has a negative intrinsic (minimum) value of $4, but the warrant might have a dollar value of say $1 because of an expected rise in common stock value.

You may use the leveraging effect to boost your dollar returns. Let's say that you have $7,000 to invest. If you purchase common stock when the market price is $35 a share, you can buy 200 shares. If the price increases to $41 a share, you will have a capital gain of $1,200. But if you invest the $7,000 in warrants priced at only $7 a share, you can acquire 1,000 of them. (One warrant equals one share.) If the price of the warrants increases by $6, your profit will be $6,000. In this instance you earn a return of only 17.1% on the common stock investment whereas on the warrants you get a return of 85.7%.

On the other hand, assume the price of the stock drops by $6. If you invest in the common stock you will lose $1,200 for a remaining equity of $5,800. However, if you invest in the warrant you will lose everything (assuming no warrant premium exists).

If an investor is to get maximum price potential from a warrant, the market price of the common stock must equal or exceed the warrant's exercise price. Also, lower-priced issues offer greater leverage opportunity. Furthermore, a warrant with a low unit price generates higher price volatility and less downside risk, and thus is preferable to a warrant with a high unit price.

Warrants can be used to *protect a speculative transaction*. For example, assume an investor sells a stock short and the price rises. The speculator cannot keep the short position continually open, and it may be too costly to wait till the stock goes down. To protect the short sale the investor may purchase a warrant fixing the purchase price and limiting the potential loss on the trade.

Assume that you sell short 100 shares at $15 each. Then you buy warrants for 100 shares at $13 a share. The cost of the option is $3, or 3 points a share, a total of $300. In effect, you are buying the stock at $16 a share. Thus, if the stock rises above $15, your loss is limited to $1 a share.

Here are some of the advantages of warrants:

- The price change in a warrant follows that of the related common stock, making a capital gain possible.
- The low unit cost allows the investor to obtain a leverage opportunity in the form of lowering the capital investment without damaging the investment's capital appreciation. This increases the potential return.
- Lower downside risk potential exists because of the lower unit price.

These are the disadvantages of warrants:

- If no price appreciation occurs before the expiration date, the warrant loses its value.

- The warrant holder receives no dividends.
- Investment in warrants requires extensive study and experience.

Calls and Puts

Calls and puts are another type of stock option. You can buy or sell them in round lots, usually 100 shares.

When you purchase a *call*, you are buying the right to purchase stock at a fixed price. You do this when you expect the price of that stock to rise. In buying a call you stand a chance of making a significant gain from a small investment, but you also risk losing your full investment if the stock does not rise in price. Calls come in bearer negotiable form and have a life of one month to nine months.

Purchasing a *put* gives you the right to sell stock at a fixed price. You might buy a put when you expect a stock price to fall. By purchasing a put you get an opportunity to make a considerable gain from a small investment, but you will lose the entire investment if the stock price does not fall. Like calls, puts come in bearer negotiable form and have a life of one month to nine months.

Calls and puts are typically written for widely held and actively traded stock on organized exchanges. Options can be traded for speculative or conservative purposes. Commissions and transaction costs are involved when a call or put is purchased or sold or written. Brokerage fees depend on the amount and value of the option contract. For instance, a contract with a value ranging from $100 to $800 has a fee of about $25.

With calls there are no voting privileges, ownership interest, or dividend income. However, option contracts are adjusted for stock splits and stock dividends.

The life of calls and puts is shorter than that of warrants but longer than that of rights. They are similar to warrants in that they are an alternative investment to common stock, leverage opportunity, and speculative investment.

Calls and puts are not issued by the company with the common stock but rather by option makers or option writers. The maker of the option receives the price paid for the call or put minus commission costs. The option trades on the open market. Calls and puts are written and can be acquired through brokers and dealers. The writer is required to purchase or deliver the stock when requested.

Holders of calls and puts do not necessarily have to exercise them to earn a return. They can trade them in the secondary market for whatever their value is. The value of a call increases as the underlying common stock goes up in price. The call can be sold on the market before its expiration date.

Calls and puts are traded on listed option exchanges, which are secondary markets like the Chicago Board Options Exchange, American Stock Exchange, Philadelphia Stock Exchange, and Pacific Stock Exchange. Figure 9.1 shows the most active options on a given day. They are also traded in the over-the-counter market. Option exchanges deal only in the purchase and sale of call and put options. *Listed options* are options traded on organized exchanges.

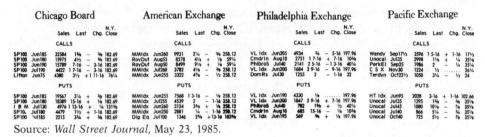

Source: *Wall Street Journal*, May 23, 1985.

Figure 9.1 *Most Active Options*

Figure 9.2 shows the growth in activity of listed options. *Conventional options* are those options traded in the over-the-counter market.

The Options Clearing Corporation issues calls listed on the options exchanges. Orders are placed with this corporation, which then issues the calls or closes the position. No certificates are issued for options, so the investor must have a brokerage account. When a holder exercises a call, he goes through the Clearing Corporation, which picks at random a writer from member accounts. A call writer would be required to sell 100 shares of the common stock at the exercise price.

Exchanges permit general orders (i.e., limit) and orders applicable only to options (i.e., spread order).

The price per share for 100 shares, which the purchaser may buy at (call), is referred to as the *striking price* (exercise price). For a put, it is the price at which the stock may be sold. The purchase or sale of the stock is to the writer of the option. The striking price is set for the life of the option on the options exchange. When stock price changes, new exercise prices are introduced for trading purposes reflecting the new value.

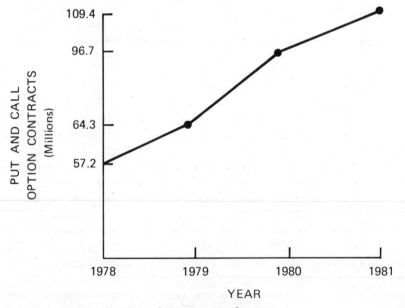

Figure 9.2 *Trend in Listed Options Trading*

In the case of conventional calls, restrictions do not exist on what the striking price should be. However, it is usually close to the market price of the stock it relates to. But in the case of listed calls, stocks having a price lower than $50 a share must have striking prices in $5 increments. Stocks between $50 and $100 have striking prices with $10 increments. Stocks higher than $100 will have striking prices in $20 increments. Striking prices are adjusted for material stock splits and stock dividends.

The expiration date of an option is the last day it can be exercised. For conventional options, the expiration date can be any business day; for a listed option there is a standardized expiration date.

The cost of an option is referred to as a *premium*. It is the price the purchaser of the call or put has to pay the writer. (With other securities, the premium is the excess of the purchase price over a determined theoretical value.)

The premium for a call depends on:

- The dividend trend of the related security
- The volume of trading in the option
- The exchange on which the option is listed
- The variability in price of the related security (A higher variability means a higher premium because of the greater speculative appeal of the option.)
- Prevailing interest rates
- The market price of the stock it relates to
- The width of the spread in price of the stock relative to the option's exercise price (A wider spread means a higher price.)
- The amount of time remaining before the option's expiration date (The longer the period the greater the premium's value.)

When the market price exceeds the strike price, the call is said to be in-the-money. But when the market price is less than the strike price, the call is out-of-the-money. Call options in-the-money have an intrinsic value equal to the difference between the market price and the strike price.

Value of call = (market price of stock – exercise price of call) × 100

For example, assume that the market price of a stock is $45, with a strike price of $40. The call has a value of $500.

Out-of-the-money call options have no intrinsic value.

If the total premium (option price) of an option is $7 and the intrinsic value is $3, there is an additional premium of $4 arising from other considerations. In effect, the total premium consists of the intrinsic value plus speculative premium (time value) based on factors such as risk, variability, forecasted future prices, expiration date, leverage, and dividend.

Total premium = intrinsic value + speculative premium

The definition of in-the-money and out-of-the-money are different for puts because puts permit the owner to sell stock at the strike price. When strike price exceeds market price of stock, we have an in-the-money put option. Its value is determined as follows:

Value of put = (exercise price of put – market price of stock) × 100

Assume the market price of a stock is $53 and the strike price of the put is $60. The value of the put is $700.

When market price of stock exceeds strike price, there is an out-of-the-money put. Because a stock owner can sell it for a greater amount in the market than he could get by exercising the put, there is no intrinsic value of the out-of-money put.

	XYZ Calls at 50 Strike Price *Stock Price*	XYZ Puts at 50 Strike Price *Stock Price*
In-the-money	Over 50	Under 50
At-the-money	50	50
Out-of-the-money	Under 50	Over 50

The theoretical value for calls and puts indicate the price at which the options should be traded. But typically they are traded at prices higher than true value when options have a long period to go. This difference is referred to as *investment premium*.

$$\text{Investment premium} = \frac{\text{option premium} - \text{option value}}{\text{option value}}$$

For example, a put has a theoretical value of $1,500 and a price of $1,750. It is therefore traded at an investment premium of 16.67%.

Calls

The *call purchaser* takes the risk of losing the entire price he or she paid for the option if a price increase does not incur. For example, assume a two-month call option allows you to acquire 500 shares of XYZ Company at $20 per share. Within that time period, you exercise the option when the market price is $38. You make a gain of $9,000 before paying the brokerage commission. If the market price had declined from $20 you would not have exercised the call option, and you would have lost the cost of the option.

By buying a call you can own common stock for a fraction of the cost of purchasing regular shares. Calls cost significantly less than common stock. Leverage is obtained because a little change in common stock price can result in a major change in the call option's price. An element of the percentage gain in the price of the call is the speculative premium attributable to the remaining time left on the call. Calls can also be viewed as a means of controlling 100 shares of stock without a large dollar investment.

Significant percentage gains on call options are possible from the low investment compared to the price of the related common stock. For example, a stock has a present market price of $35. A call can be purchased for $300 allowing the acquisition of 100 shares at $35 each. If the price of the stock increases, the call will also be worth more. Assume that the stock is at $55 at the call's expiration date. The profit is $20 on each of the 100 shares of stock in the call, or a total of $2,000 on an investment of $300. A return of 667% is thus earned. In effect, when the holder exercises the call for 100 shares at $35 each, he or she can immediately sell them at $55 per share. Note that the investor could have earned the same amount by investing directly in the common stock, but the investment would have been $3,500 so the rate of return would have been significantly lower.

You can buy AB Company stock at $30 a share, or $3,000 for 100 shares. You can acquire a $33 three-month call for $400. Thus, you could invest $2,600 cash and have opportunity to buy 100 shares at $33. Assume, however, that you decide to invest your $2,600 in a three-month CD earning 14% interest. The CD will return $91 (14% × $2,600 × 3/12). If the AB Company stock goes to $16, the option will be worthless but the significant loss on the stock of $14 a share did not occur. Rather, the loss is limited to $309 ($400 – $91). However, note that by not buying a stock you may have foregone a dividend.

If the stock went up to $43, the call would be exercised at $33 resulting in a sizable gain with little investment.

Here is another example of call trading. Let's say that a call gives you the right to acquire 100 shares of $30 stock at $27. The call will trade at a price of about $3 a share. Call options may also be used when you believe the stock price will increase in the future but you have a cash flow problem and are unable to buy the stock. However, you will have sufficient cash to do so later. In this situation, you can buy a call so as not to lose a good investment opportunity. For example, on Februry 6 you purchase a $32 June call option for $3 a share. If the stock has a market price of $34½, the speculative premium is $½. In June, you exercise the call option when the stock price is $37. The cost of the 100 shares of stock for tax reporting is the strike price ($32) plus the option premium ($3), or $35.

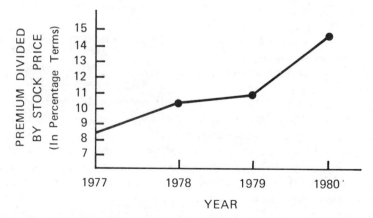

Figure 9.3 *Trend in Chicago Board Options Exchange*
Call Option Index

Puts

The *put holder* may sell 100 shares at the strike price for a given period to a put writer. A put is purchased when there is an anticipation of a price decline. The maximum loss is the premium cost (investment), which will be lost if the price of the stock does not drop.

Let's suppose that a stock has a market price of $35. You acquire a put to sell 100 shares of stock at $35 per share. The cost of the put is $300. At the exercise date of the put, the price of the stock goes to $15 a share. You therefore realize a profit of $20 per share, or $2,000. As the holder of the put, you simply buy on the market 100 shares at $15 each and then sell them to the writer of the put for $35 each. The net gain is $1,700.

To further illustrate this, assume that TUV stock's price was $55 on March 2. You buy a $56 June put for $4. The speculative premium is therefore $3. On June 7, the stock price falls to $47 and the price of the June $56 put to $8. The intrinsic value is $9 and the speculative premium is $1. As the put holder, you now have a gain of $4.

Call and Put Investment Strategies

The investment approaches one can take with calls and puts include hedging, speculation, straddles, and spreads.

Owners of call and put options can *hedge* by holding on to two or more securities to lower risk and at the same time make some profit. It may involve buying a stock and later purchasing an option on it. For example, a stock may be bought along with writing a call on it. Also, a holder of a stock that has risen in price may buy a put to furnish downside risk protection.

As an example of hedging, let's say that you buy 100 shares of XYZ at $26 each and a put for $200 on the 100 shares at an exercise price of $26. If the stock remains static, you will lose $200 on the put. If the price decreases, your loss on the stock will be offset by your gain on the put. If stock price rises, you'll earn a capital gain on the stock and lose your investment in the put. In other words, to get the benefit of a hedge, you have to incur a loss on the put. (Also note that at expiration of the put, you incur a loss with no further hedge.)

You can also buy a put to hedge your position after making a profit on the stock. For example, let's say you hold 100 shares of XYZ stock purchased at $60 a share. That stock increases to $80, earning a profit of $20 a share. To guarantee your profit you buy a put with an $80 exercise price at a cost of $300. No matter what happens later, you will have a minimum gain of $1,700. If the stock price falls, your minimum profit will be $1,700, but if the stock price rises, you'll realize an additional profit. Some other time you might buy a call to protect a short sale from the risk of increasing stock price. By doing this, you hedge your position as follows: when you use a call, you as a short seller will not suffer a loss in excess of a given amount. However, you have lowered your profit by the cost of the call.

Calls and puts may also be used for *speculation* as an alternative to investment in the related stocks. The idea is buy low and sell high. You would acquire options when you think you will earn a higher return than you would by investing in the underlying stock. In general, you can obtain a higher return rate at lower risk with out-of-the-money options. The problem with an out-of-money option is that price consists only of the investment premium, which you can lose if the stock does not rise.

Here is an example of this kind of speculation. A speculator purchases an option contract to buy 100 shares at $25 a share. The option costs $150. Assume a rise in stock price to $33 a share. The speculator exercises the option and sells the shares in the market, realizing a gain of $650 ($33 – $25 – $1.50 = $6.50 × 100 shares). Now the speculator can sell the option in the market and make a profit because of its increased value. However, if there is a decline in stock price, the loss to the holder is limited to $150 (the option's cost). Of course, brokerage fees are also involved. In effect, this call option permitted the speculator to purchase 100 shares worth $2,500 for $150 for a short period.

Straddling integrates a put and call on the same stock with the identical strike price and exercise date. It is used by a speculator trading on both sides of the market. This speculator hopes for significant movement in stock price in one direction so as to make a gain that exceeds the cost of both options. If the price movement does not go as expected, however, the loss will equal the cost of the options. The straddle holder may widen risk and profit potential by closing one option before closing the other.

For example, you buy a call and put for $4 each on September 30 when the stock price is $42. The expiration period is four months. The investment is $8, or $800 in total. Assume the stock increases to $60 at expiration of the options. The call earns a profit of $14 ($18 – $4) and the loss on the put is $4. Your net gain is $10, or $1,000 all together.

A *spread* is the purchase of an option (long position) and the writing of an option (short position) in the same security, using call options. Sophisticated investors may write many spreads to gain from the differences in option premiums. Return potential is significant, but the risk is very high. There are different types of spreads:

- A *vertical spread* is the purchase and writing of two contracts at different striking prices with the same expiration date.
- A *horizontal spread* is the purchase and writing of two options with the same strike price but for different periods.
- A *diagonal spread* combines the horizontal and vertical.

Spreads require the investor to buy one call and sell another call. The gain or loss from a spread position depends on the change between two option prices as the price of the stock increases or decreases. The difference between two option prices is the *price spread*.

The speculator who uses a vertical bull spread anticipates an increase in price of stock, but this strategy reduces the risk. Here there is a ceiling on the gain or loss.

A speculator using a vertical bear spread expects the stock price to decline. This investor sells short the call with the lower strike price and places a cap on upside risk by buying a call with a higher strike price.

Puts, straddles, and spreads may be bought either to maximize return or to minimize risk. They are not traded on listed exchanges but rather must be acquired through brokerage houses and members of the Put and Call Brokers and Dealers Association.

Those who employ straddles, spreads, and other similar strategies often use extensive computer analysis. These investment approaches should be left to very sophisticated investors.

Option Writing

The writer of a call agrees to sell shares at the strike price for the price paid for the call option. Call option writers do the opposite of what buyers do. Investors write options because they believe that a price increase in the stock will be less than what the call purchaser expects. They may even expect the price of the stock to remain static or to decrease. Option writers receive the option premium minus related transaction costs. So if the option is not exercised the writer earns the price paid for it. However, when an option is exercised, the writer suffers a loss, sometimes quite a significant one.

When the writer of an option decides to sell shares, he or she must come up with stock at the agreed-upon price if the option is exercised. In either case, the option writer receives income from the premium. (Shares are sold in denominations of 100.) An investor usually sells an option when he or she expects it not to be exercised. The risk of option writing is that the writer, if uncovered, must buy stock or, if covered, loses the gain.

As the writer, you can buy back an option to terminate your exposure. For example, assume the strike price is $40 and the premium for the call option is $5. If the stock is at less than $40, the call would not be exercised, and you would earn the premium of $5. If the stock exceeds $40, the call may be exercised, and you must provide 100 shares at $40. However, the call writer would lose money only if the stock price exceeded $45.

Options may be *naked (uncovered)* or *covered. Naked options* are options on stock that the writer does not own. The investor writes the call or put for the premium and will keep it if the price change is in his favor or immaterial in amount. But the writer's loss exposure is unlimited. *Covered option* are written against stocks the writer owns and are not quite as risky. For example, a call can be written for stock the writer owns or a put can be written for stock sold short. This is a conservative mechanism to obtain positive returns. The goal is to write an out-of-the-money option, keep the premium paid, and have the market price of the stock equal but not exceed the option exercise price. Writing a covered call option is similar to hedging a position since if stock price falls, the writer's loss on the stock is partly netted against the option premium.

Review

1.   What is a stock right?

_____

an option allowing stockholders to buy new common stock at a subscription price, usually below market price, for a given period

2. **(T,F)** A brokerage commission is involved in a stock right.

_____

False

3. How long is a stock right usually open?

_____

several weeks

4. **(T,F)** Unwanted stock rights can be sold.

_____

True

5. Your right as an existing stockholder to maintain your fractional interest in the business when new common stock is floated is known as the _____ right.

_____

preemptive

6. What is a rights-on trade?

_____

one in which stock is traded with rights attached

7. What is an ex-right?

_____

a right purchased and sold separately from the underlying stock

8. What is a warrant?

_____

the option to buy a given number of shares for a specified period at a subscription price that is higher than the current market price of the stock

9. **(T,F)** Warrants are often issued along with corporate bonds to attract investors.

_____

True

10. **(T,F)** Warrants offer the investor a capital gain potential in return for a limited investment.

_____

True

11. Which remains in effect longer, a right or a warrant?

_____

a warrant

12. How are warrants related to bond issues?

___

They are often offered as sweeteners to bond issues.

13. Which one of the following statements is true?
  a. Warrants may not be issued with preferred stock.
  b. Warrants are not traded on the exchanges.
  c. Some warrants have no maturity date.
  d. Most warrants are callable.

___

c

14. Which one of the following statements is false?
  a. A warrant is used to buy a bond at a later date.
  b. Most warrants are detachable from the bond once issued.
  c. Warrants can be transacted on margin.
  d. When warrants are issued, the exercise (subscription) price exceeds the maket price.

___

a

15. Which of the following statements is false?
  a. Dividends are paid on warrants.
  b. Most warrants are traded on the American Stock Exchange.
  c. Warrant holders cannot vote.
  d. Warrants provide a leverage opportunity.

___

a

16. List some of the advantages of investing in warrants.

___

capital gain potential
low unit cost
leveraging effect
an increase in value as the price of the underlying stock rises

17. Generally speaking, why is the investor willing to pay less for a warrant as the price of the underlying common stock rises?

___

There is a loss in leverage as stock price moves upward. Also, if stock price falls, less downside protection exists.

18. Which one of the following statements is true?
    a. Puts and calls are issued by the company floating the underlying common stock.
    b. Options are usually written for widely held and active stocks.
    c. The holder of an option will receive a cash dividend on it.
    d. Options are not adjusted for stock dividends.

    b

19. What variables affect the price of an option?

    anticipated trends in the market, price vacillation of the stock, dividend return on the stock, time period remaining, and leveraging effect

20. What is the striking price?

    the price of 100 shares, which is fixed for the life of the stock

21. What is an option premium?

    the price paid by the buyer to the writer for a call or put

22. What is indicated by the speculative premium of a put as a percent of the stock price?

    the percentage drop in price of stock required for the owner of the put to break even

23. How does an in-the-money option differ from an out-of-the-money option?

    An in-the-money option takes place when the exercise price is less than the market price of the stock. If the exercise price exceeds the market price of the stock, you have an out-of-the-money situation.

24. (T,F) Leverage in a call occurs when the percentage price increase in the option is greater than the percentage price increase in the stock.

    True

25. (T,F) You may buy a call if you believe stock price will later rise and you currently have a cash flow problem.

    True

26. Which of the following statements is true?
  a. A put can be used to buy a security.
  b. Calls and puts cannot be sold in the secondary market.
  c. High beta stocks have a lower speculative premium.
  d. An investor who does not exercise a put option loses all of his or her investment.

d

27. When you purchase a stock and acquire a put on it, you are _____ your position.

hedging

28. What is a straddle?

A straddle combines a call and put on the identical stock with the same expiration date and strike price. It is employed to take advantage of significant variability in stock price. High beta stocks might be most suited for this. A significant price movement on one side will cover the cost of obtaining the options.

29. What is a spread?

A spread is buying an option (long position) and writing an option (short position) on the same security.

30. (T,F) The maker of an option writes it.

True

31. What is the difference between a naked option and a covered option?

The writer of a naked option is not an owner in the shares at the time the call is written. The writer of a covered option is the owner of the shares.

32. (T,F) The writer of a naked call option anticipates a stock price increase.

False

Self-Test

1. Which one of the following statements about stock rights is false?
  a. No brokerage fee is involved.
  b. No secondary market exists.

    c.   The time span is short.

    d.   The subscription price is set below the present market price.

2. Present stockholders' right to acquire new share issuances in order to maintain their percentage ownership interest is known as the _____ right.

3. (**T,F**) Stock rights cannot be sold in a secondary market.

4. When stock is traded with rights attached, it is called a _____ sale.

5. What is an ex-right?

6. How is the value of a right determined?

7. Which of the following statements about stock warrants is false?

    a.   A stock warrant has a life of several years.

    b.   Option price is established above the present market price of a stock.

    c.   Stock warrants are often used as sweeteners to bond issues.

    d.   Stock warrants do not apply to preferred stock.

8. The life of a warrant is _____ than the life of a stock right.

9. (**T,F**) Warrants exist for all securities.

10. Which one of the following statements about warrants is true?

    a.   No secondary market for warrants exists.

    b.   Holders of warrants have voting rights.

    c.   Warrants can be purchased on margin.

    d.   Warrants never have a maturity date.

11. Which statement about warrants is false?

    a.   Warrants have a leverage effect.

    b.   Holders of warrants receive a cash dividend.

    c.   Warrants can provide a capital gain.

    d.   The value of warrants is tied to that of related common stock.

12. What does the term "premium" mean as applied to a warrant?

13. You pay $16,000 for warrants having a unit price of $8. One warrant equals one share. The warrant increases to $12.

    a.   How many warrants did you acquire?

    b.   What rate of return did you earn?

14. If you do not exercise the warrant in question 13, what value is assigned to it?

15. You sell at $30 a warrant that cost $14. The holding period is three years. What is the rate of return?

16. A warrant allows you to purchase one share of common stock at $55 per share. The current market price is $63. The warrant sells for $10.

    a.   What is the intrinsic value?

    b.   What is the premium?

17. One warrant equals one share. The exercise price is $12. The market price of the stock is $16. The warrants are traded at $5. Determine the percentage premium.

18. Market price of common stock is $50. The exercise price of the warrant is $32. Six warrants equal one share. The warrants are selling at 40% premium. At what price will the warrant trade?

19. (**T,F**) A warrant can help offset the adverse effect of a short sale.

20. (**T,F**) Options can be traded in the secondary market.

21. **(T,F)** Options are in bearer form.
22. Options are traded in terms of _____ lots of (typically) _____shares.
23. What is the usual maturity of an option?
24. **(T,F)** An option usually has a shorter life than a warrant does.
25. What is a put?
26. What does an option writer do?
27. **(T,F)** If you hold a call option and the company pays a cash dividend, you will receive it.
28. Option contracts are adjusted for _____ and _____.
29. Options traded in the over-the-counter market are known as _____ options.
30. The _____ acts as the issuer of calls listed on the options exchange.
31. Which of the following statements is false?
    a. A call is an alternative to investing in common stocks.
    b. A call is a speculative investment.
    c. A call has a life of no more than one year.
    d. Calls offer leverage opportunity.
32. What is the striking price?
33. Stocks with a price of less than $50 have striking prices in $_____ increments.
34. **(T,F)** Listed options have standardized expiration dates.
35. What is an option premium?
36. An option premium does *not* depend on
    a. expiration period of option
    b. foreign currency exchange rate
    c. trading volume
    d. stability in stock price
37. When market price is below the strike price, the call is said to be _____.
38. **(T,F)** The return on an option comes solely from capital appreciation.
39. If you do not exercise a call option, you will lose your _____.
40. If stock price increases, who will have a greater percentage return—the holder of a call or the holder of the related stock?
41. **(T,F)** If a bear market is expected, you should buy a call.
42. When does the writer of a call option profit?
43. What is a naked option?

Self-Test Answers

1. b
2. preemptive
3. False
4. rights-on
5. a right that is bought and sold separately from the stock

6. $$\frac{\text{Market price of current stock} - \text{subscription price of new stock}}{\text{Number of rights to purchase one share}}$$

7. d

8. longer

9. False

10. c

11. b

12. the amount by which the value of a warrant on the market exceeds its intrinsic value

13. a. $\dfrac{\$16,000}{\$8} = 2,000$ warrants

 b. $\dfrac{\$4 \times 2,000}{\$16,000} = \dfrac{\$8,000}{\$16,000} = 50\%$

14. 0

15. $$\frac{\dfrac{\$30 - \$14}{3}}{\dfrac{\$30 + \$14}{2}} = \frac{\$5.33}{\$8.00} = 66.7\%$$

16. a. $(\$63 - \$55) \times 1 = \$8$
 b. $\$10 - \$8 = \$2$

17. $(\$16 - \$12) \times 1 = \$4$

 Premium $= (\$5 - \$4) = \$1$

 Percentage Premium $= \dfrac{\$1}{\$4} = 25\%$

18. $(\$50 - \$32) \times \dfrac{1}{6} = \$3$

 Premium $= \$3 \times 1.4 = \$4.20$

19. True

20. True

21. True

22. round, 100

23. 30 days to 9 months

24. True

25. A put is the option to sell common shares at a set price by a specified date. The put holder anticipates a decline in stock price.

26. The option writer makes the option and buys or delivers the stock to the option holders.

27. False

28. stock splits, stock dividends

29. conventional

30. Options Clearing Corporation

31. c

32. the price per share to buy 100 shares under a call

33. $5

34. True

35. the price paid for an option

36. b

37. out-of-the-money

38. True

39. entire investment

40. the holder of the call

41. False

42. The call option writer earns in full the price of the call paid by the investor if stock price does not increase enough for the call investor to exercise it.

43. A naked option is an option on stock the writer does not own at the time the call is written.

TANGIBLE INVESTMENTS 10
Precious Metals, Collectibles, and Real Estate _____

Objectives

When you complete this chapter, you will be able to:

- Discuss the characteristics, suitability, and advantages of real asset investments
- Explain how to make tangible investments
- List the circumstances in which investment in gold and silver are appropriate
- Enumerate the various precious gems in which one can invest
- Identify the advantages of investing in collectibles
- List the various types of real estate investment and the advantages and disadvantages of each
- Explain mortgage terms

What Are Tangible Assets?

Tangible assets, or real assets, can be touched and owned. Examples include precious metals, gems, collectibles, and real estate. Most people own one or more of these assets, or would like to. The only return from most tangible assets is capital appreciation. An exception, of course, is real estate that provides rental income.

- In inflation, they have done better than stocks and other financial investments.

159

- They do better in troubled times when uncertainty exists in investors' minds.
- Tangible assets help to diversify a portfolio because they usually go up in value when financial assets are going down and vice versa.
- Some real assets provide aesthetic or personal pleasure as well as financial security.

The disadvantages of real assets are these:

- There is not always a secondary market for them; in other words, they have low liquidity.
- The dealer spread applicable to real assets can be 25% or more, whereas the commission associated with financial assets is only about 2%. (The percent spread for real assets with low value can be quite high; with more valuable items, the percent spread declines.)
- Investors in real assets may have to pay for storage and insurance.
- Except for rental real estate, tangible assets provide no current income.

Precious Metals

Precious metals include gold and silver. They are liquid; they have international markets; and they provide a hedge against inflation. However, precious metals are an unstable investment. The prices typically increase in difficult periods and decline in stable ones. They are not periodically taxed like real estate, but the investor must pay a long-term capital gains tax after selling these assets at a profit.

Gold

Gold is a valuable commodity representing a private store of value. It is measured in troy ounces. Gold is an inflation hedge and is a good investment when paper currency is depreciating and when interest rates are low. In fact, low interest rates will prompt investment in gold because other forms of investment are yielding low returns. Gold for investment purposes may take the following forms: jewelry, coins, bullion, certificates, shares of a mining business, and futures.

Gold usually does the opposite of common stock: As common stock returns move down, returns on gold move up. In other words, gold compensates for a declining stock market. Transaction costs for gold vary with the type of gold, but the higher the quantity purchased, the lower the percentage commission.

You can purchase gold *coins* from post offices, banks, and gold dealers. Gold coins differ in price depending on quality and content. Commissions typically vary between 2% and 4%. Coins are easily marketable and movable.

You can also buy gold bullion in bars through banks and dealers. Dealer markups and commissions range from 3% to 10%, depending on the quantity purchased. Assaying—testing for gold content—may be necessary. Or you could purchase a gold certificate as evidence of your ownership in a given number of gold ounces stored in a bank safe. These gold certificates are not always subject to the state sales tax that applies to bullion. Also, you don't have to worry about losing the gold or having it stolen, because it remains in the bank.

You can acquire indirect ownership by purchasing *shares in a gold mine*. However, the prices of shares do not always move in the same manner as the price of the gold itself. Securities of gold mines do enhance portfolio diversification, though, in the same way that the metal itself does. Mining company stocks are traded on organized exchanges and in the over-the-counter market. Most gold mines are located in South Africa.

You can also acquire *shares of mutual funds* maintaining a strong position in gold stocks or gold bullion. Mutual fund investment offers diversification. *Gold futures* can be bought on some commodities exchanges. You need give only about 10% in cash of the contract's value to buy. This low margin requirement provides a leveraging opportunity. Commissions typically are less than 1% of the contract's value. Gold futures are traded in several U.S. and foreign exchanges.

Gold ownership has several disadvantages:

- Storage costs for gold are high.
- High transaction costs are common.
- Investors receive no dividend revenue on gold, and capital gain or loss potential is significant.
- Significant price volatility results in a high degree of risk. Variability in price is partly due to changes in the international market emanating typically from such factors as speculation.
- Certain gold investments (e.g., bullion and coins) are in bearer form. If they are lost or stolen, the owner loses the entire investment. (Gold shares or certificates are protected by registration.)

Silver

Silver may take the form of bars, coins, jewelry, and flatware. Futures contracts also exist for silver. They are traded on some commodities exchanges. The return from pure silver investment (not stocks) is the capital gain from increased value. Silver is significantly lower in price than gold, but you must buy more of it, and so the carrying cost is relatively high.

Stock prices of silver mining companies depend on the price of silver and also on the financial health of the companies themselves.

Historical interest requires mention of the Hunt silver scandal. The Hunt Brothers and other speculators purchased 300 million ounces of silver resulting in a price increase from $6.50 an ounce in January 1979 to $50.35 an ounce in January 1980. Difficulties arose when the purchasers demanded delivery of the silver. The inability of the Hunt Brothers to meet the margin requirements on their tremendous investment resulted in a great deterioration in the price of silver as well as other commodities and stocks. Also, silver market trading activity dropped drastically.

Gems and Collectibles

Precious gems include diamonds and rubies. They have the advantage of being durable, small, and easily hidden and transported; also, they have significant potential for price increase. One major drawback, however, is price volatility depending on market conditions. Another is that great expertise is needed for successful investment.

Collectibles include rare stamps, art, books, and valuable coins and jewelry. Acquisition occurs through dealers, auction, or directly from previous owners. Drawbacks to ownership in collectibles include:

- High insurance cost
- There is usually an absence of immediate marketability. Resale markets for different items vary and have significant transaction fees.
- Possible forgeries

Table 10.1 lists precious metals and collectibles in terms of their return rates, from highest to lowest.

Table 10.1 **Return Rates from Highest to Lowest for Precious Metals and Collectibles**

Stamps
Silver
Coins
Diamonds

Real Estate

You can own real estate in the form of

- A home
- Residential property (e.g., apartment house)
- Commercial property (i.e., office building, shopping center)
- Raw land
- Limited partnership in a real estate syndicate
- Ownership of shares in a real estate investment trust (REIT)

Real estate property provides for capital appreciation. Certain real estate investment property—residential and commercial property, for example—generates annual income. Before investing in real estate, you should consider the risk/return trade-off associated with the different types. Investors with sufficient funds can purchase real estate directly. Those with limited funds can make an indirect investment in REITS, real estate tax shelters, and mortgage-related securities.

Brokerage firms are now investing in real estate. Brokerage houses like Merrill Lynch have real estate affiliates, engage in mortgage banking, and handle real estate syndications. Institutional investors also invest in real estate. Mutual funds are involved as well. For example, T. Rowe Price charges no sales commission.

Advantages of real estate investment include the following:

- Means of building an equity (estate). High yields can be gotten from real estate.

- Tax benefits. The capital gain on the sale of real estate has favorable tax treatment. Also, real estate income property provides an excellent tax shelter because of the deductibility of depreciation expense in addition to the usual interest expense and property taxes. The tax savings of course increases with the owner's tax rate.
- Inflation hedge. Increased value in real estate has typically exceeded the rate of inflation. But it has to be noted that real estate as a hedge against inflation varies from area to area, based on local real estate price inflation.
- Leverage. Leverage exists with real estate since a high percentage of the investment may be made with debt funds. Down payments are often less than 25%. Leverage enhances earnings when the return earned on borrowed funds exceeds the after-tax interest cost. Huge rates of return are possible when significant capital appreciation takes place on the limited down payment. However, leverage increases investment risk, since foreclosure will occur if the borrowed funds are not repaid.

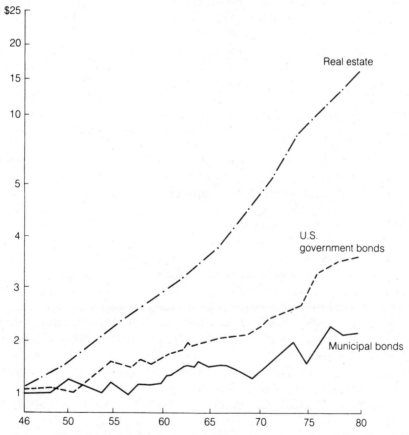

Source: "Soaring Real Estate Values Are Enticing Big Securities Concerns into the Field," *Wall Street Journal*, August 6, 1980, p. 32.

Figure 10.1 *Comparison of Change in Real Estate Value Relative to Government Securities*

- Pride of ownership
- Good collateral for a loan
- Government assistance exists (e.g., Veterans Administration loan guarantees)

Some disadvantages of real estate investing are:

- Government regulation such as zoning requirements and building codes
- High property taxes
- Possible losses if property declines in value

In effect, *homeowners* are investing in real estate. Tax benefits from home ownership include deductible interest expense on mortgage and property taxes. Also, only 40% of the capital gain on the sale of property is subject to tax. The capital gain on the sale of a house is deferred and reduces the cost basis of the new home if the homeowner reinvests in another house of equal or a greater value within eighteen months of the sale. Further, there is a one-time tax-free gain allowed on the sale of real estate worth $100,000 when the seller is fifty-five or older. Reinvestment is not required in a new home.

Considering the after-tax effect, the cost of a home is not significantly higher than the cost of renting. But taking into account capital appreciation of the house, home ownership is considerably more financially advantageous. However, expenses such as insurance and maintenance should be considered.

Investing in real estate (i.e., land, cooperative apartment) as an individual is a simple means of real estate ownership. You are in control. Since control is easily delineated, immediate corrective action may be taken. Drawbacks are restrictions on capital to expand and a lack of expertise. Unlimited liability also exists.

Commercial and industrial properties (e.g., office building, shopping center) have varying degrees of risk depending on the occupants. Operating expenses applicable to rental property include property taxes, maintenance, insurance, utilities, and management fees.

Raw (undeveloped) land has the greatest risk but possesses the highest return potential. Annual income is virtually nonexistent. Return is solely capital gain. Land does not depreciate so tax deductibility for depreciation does not apply.

REITs issue shares to obtain invested capital, which along with borrowed funds is placed in long-term mortgages and real estate projects. REITs are similar to mutual funds and are traded on the exchanges or over-the-counter. Here, the small investor can get involved. But it is difficult from a distance to judge the true value of underlying assets in a real estate trust. REITs are a liquid investment because there is a secondary market for shares.

There is a single taxation of income since the trust does not pay the tax but only the taxpayer. REITs have to distribute their earnings to investors. A form is sent to the taxpayer each year indicating the income to be recognized on the individual's tax return.

REITs are formed by and associated with financial institutions such as the Bank America Realty. An example of a REIT is General Growth Properties.

REITs are of the following types:

- Mortgage trusts, which furnish long-term loans to investors in real estate
- Equity trusts, which purchase, operate, and sell real estate as an investment

- Construction and development trusts, which give short-term loans to developers for construction

A *real estate syndicate* (limited partnership) is a tax-sheltered investment with potential for significant gain. The *general partner* is the decisionmaker as to property investment and management. He or she also has the entire liability. The general partner can be one or more individuals or a corporation. This partner sells participation units to *limited partners* (whose obligations are usually limited to their investments). Ownership can be in future unnamed properties (a blind pool) or in specific existing ones. The buyer should beware that in many cases general partners have made substantial sums by buying properties themselves and then selling them to the other partners. In addition to general partner and limited partner cash investments, debt is often undertaken to acquire properties.

A public limited partnership exists where the minimum investment is greatly less than the minimum investment required with a private offering. A public offering is registered with the SEC.

The general partner determines the payout to all partners but usually hires a manager to handle the affairs of the real estate holding.

Tax benefit comes in the form of depreciation and interest deductibility. For partners in or above the 40% tax bracket, recognizing tax losses in the initial years of a real estate venture provides a good tax shelter. In later years, the advantage is the capital gain from sale. Profits of partnership arrangements go directly to the partners. Hence, there is no double taxation.

A limited partnership enables one to have greater and more diversified holdings relative to an individual or regular partnership. However, disadvantages of a limited partnership are:

- Limited partners have minimal control over activities.
- High fees ranging anywhere between 5% and 25% may be charged by the general partner.
- The borrowed amount if not repaid will force foreclosure.
- Limited partnership shares have no marketability because they are not traded; in other words, there is no secondary market.

When you appraise the potential of a real estate arrangement involving a general partner, you should consider the following:

- Potential litigation against the partnership
- Previous success and failure, including delays in payout to limited partners
- Whether funds are invested in unspecified future projects or in identifiable, specific ones
- Whether limited partnership investment should be publicly or privately received. A private offering is usually local and has a restricted number of investors.

Review

1. During inflation, which has generally done better—tangible investments or security investments?

tangible investments

2. **(T,F)** In troubled times, real assets usually outperform financial assets.

    True

3. The return on real assets almost always comes from _____.

    capital appreciation

4. **(T,F)** Tangibles do not provide interest or dividends.

    True

5. **(T,F)** Tangibles include collectibles, gold, silver, real estate, and diamonds.

    True

6. Do real asset investments assist in portfolio diversification?

    Yes. Real assets often do well when financial assets are doing poorly and so provide balance.

7. **(T,F)** Dealer spreads for real assets are higher than for financial assets.

    True

8. What are the disadvantages of real asset investment?

    low liquidity, high dealer spreads, storage and insurance costs, and absence of current income

9. **(T,F)** The prices of gold and silver are unstable.

    True

10. **(T,F)** Gold and silver do better in problem times than they do in stable periods.

    True

11. Gold is measured in _____.

troy ounces

12. When does gold usually increase in value?

during times of inflation, international problems, depreciation in paper currency, investor concerns, and low interest rates

13. (T,F) Futures contracts do not exist for gold.

False.

14. (T,F) Gold and common stocks behave in opposite ways.

True

15. (T,F) Silver prices are about the same as gold prices.

False

16. (T,F) Futures contracts cannot be taken out on gold and silver.

False

17. (T,F) Prices of gems and collectibles can vary.

True

18. What are the disadvantages of owning collectibles?

insurance expense, lack of marketability, and possible forgeries

19. (T,F) Of the real assets, real estate provides the greatest tax benefit.

True

20. (T,F) Real estate provides an opportunity for high leverage.

True

21. _____ of the capital gain on real estate is subject to tax if the seller does not buy a new house within _____ months.

40%, eighteen

22. **(T,F)** Undeveloped land provides the highest risk/return relationship.

_____

True

23. **(T,F)** Property taxes and interest are tax deductible, but depreciation on rental property is not.

_____

False

24. A _____ is a closed-end investment company putting funds in mortgages and real estate.

_____

REIT

25. **(T,F)** The shares of REITs are publicly traded.

_____

True

26. **(T,F)** In a real estate syndicate, a general partner has unlimited liability while a limited partner is liable only for his or her original investment.

_____

True

27. What is a blind pool?

_____

ownership in future unidentified properties

28. **(T,F)** A real estate syndicate does not incur debt.

_____

False

29. Match the investment needs with the type of real estate to be invested in.

1.	Capital appreciation	A. Rental units
2.	Current income	B. REITs
3.	Tax shelter	C. Raw land

_____

1. C
2. A
3. B

30. The only real estate investment that can be sold on a secondary market is the _____.

   REIT

Self-Test

1. Each of the following is an example of a real asset except:
   a. silver
   b. real estate
   c. diamonds
   d. bonds
2. Do tangible investments usually do better or worse than financial ones during inflationary periods and difficult times?
3. The return from each of the following is solely from capital appreciation except:
   a. commercial property
   b. gold
   c. gems
   d. collectibles
4. Which of the following is an advantage of real asset investment?
   a. diversification of portfolio
   b. price variability
   c. illiquidity
   d. storage cost
5. (T,F) Silver has an international market.
6. Gold investment may be in the form of
   a. bullion
   b. certificates
   c. futures
   d. all of the above
7. Gold is measured in _____.
8. Gold does not do very well during times of
   a. low interest rates
   b. decrease in margin requirements
   c. depreciation in paper currency
   d. worldwide crisis
9. Gold usually goes up in value when _____ go down.
10. (T,F) There is a high margin requirement on buying gold.
11. What is assaying?
12. Each of the following is a disadvantage of investments in gold except:
    a. high storage cost
    b. high transaction cost
    c. lack of annual interest income
    d. price stability
13. (T,F) Futures contracts exist for silver.

14. Each of the following is a disadvantage of investing in collectibles except:
    a. the chance of acquiring forgeries
    b. tax on annual dividend income
    c. high insurance costs
    d. lack of marketability
15. To avoid paying a capital gain tax on the sale of your house, you must buy a new house within _____ months.
16. Which of the following does not provide income?
    a. commercial property
    b. apartment house
    c. shopping center
    d. undeveloped land
17. Which real estate investment provides the greatest return potential but also has the greatest risk?
    a. commercial property
    b. undeveloped land
    c. REIT
    d. real estate syndicate
18. What is a REIT?
19. Which one of the following is not a type of REIT?
    a. equity trust
    b. construction trust
    c. mortgage trust
    d. beneficial trust
20. (T,F) A REIT must distribute current income for tax purposes.
21. In a limited partnership, the decisionmaker is the _____.
22. (T,F) The maximum fee that can be charged of limited partners is 15%.
23. If your main desire is capital appreciation, your best investment is _____.
24. The only secondary market for real estate is in _____.

Self-Test Answers

1. d
2. better
3. a
4. a
5. True
6. d
7. troy ounces
8. b
9. financial investments such as stocks and bonds
10. False
11. testing for gold content
12. d
13. True

14. b
15. eighteen
16. d
17. b
18. a real estate investment trust that issues shares to get capital investment, which along with debt is invested in long-term mortgages and real estate. There is a secondary market for shares purchased.
19. d
20. True
21. general partner
22. False
23. raw land
24. REITs

FUTURES IN COMMODITIES AND FINANCIAL INSTRUMENTS

11

Objectives

When you complete this chapter, you will be able to:

- Describe the futures market
- Enumerate the ways in which futures are used by hedgers and speculators
- Discuss the use of commodity futures
- State the reasons for using financial futures
- Determine the rate of return on various kinds of futures contracts

Futures Contracts

In the *futures market*, investors trade in commodities and financial instruments. A *future* is a contract to purchase or sell a given amount of an item for a given price by a certain date (in the future—thus the name "futures market"). The seller of a futures contract agrees to deliver the item to the buyer of the contract, who agrees to purchase the item. The contract specifies the amount, valuation, method, quality, month and means of delivery, and exchange to be traded in. The month of delivery is the expiration date; in other words, the date on which the commodity or financial instrument must be delivered. *Com-*

172

modity contracts are guarantees by a seller to deliver a commodity (e.g., cocoa or cotton). *Financial contracts* are a commitment by the seller to deliver a financial instrument (e.g., a Treasury bill) or a specific amount of foreign currency. Futures can be risky; to invest in them, you will need specialized knowledge and great caution.

A *long position* is the acquisition of a contract in the hope that its price will rise. A *short position* is selling it in anticipation of a price drop. The position may be terminated through reversing the transaction. For instance, the long buyer can later take a short position of the same amount of the commodity or financial instrument. Almost all futures are offset (canceled out) before delivery. It is rare for delivery to settle the futures contract.

Trading in futures is conducted by hedgers and speculators. *Hedgers* protect themselves with futures contracts in the commodity they produce or in the financial instrument they hold. For instance, if a producer of wheat anticipates a decline in wheat prices, he can sell a futures contract to guarantee a higher current price. Then, when future delivery is made, he will receive the higher price. *Speculators* use futures contracts to obtain capital gain on price rises of the commodity, currency, or financial instrument.

Commodity futures trading is accomplished by open outcry auction. A futures contract can be traded in the futures market. Trading is done through specialized brokers, and certain commodity firms deal only in futures. Fees for futures contracts are based on the amount of the contract and the price of the item. Commissions vary according to the amount and nature of the contract. Trading in futures is basically the same as dealing in stocks, except that the investor must establish a commodity trading account. Margin buying and kinds of orders are the same, however. And the investor can purchase or sell contracts with desired terms.

Futures trading can help an investor cope with inflation. However, as we said earlier, futures contracts are a specialized, high-risk area because of the numerous variables involved, one of which is the international economic situation. Futures contract prices can be quite volatile.

Commodities Futures

In a *commodity contract*, the seller promises to deliver a given commodity by a certain date at a predetermined price. The contract specifies the item, the price, the expiration date, and a standardized unit to be traded (e.g., 50,000 pounds). Commodity contracts may run up to one year. Investors must continually evaluate the effect of market activity on the value of the contract.

Let's say that you buy a futures contract for the delivery of 1,000 units of a commodity five months from now at $4.00 per unit. The seller of the contract does not have to have physical possession of the item, and you, as the contract buyer, need not take custody of the commodity at the "delivery" date. Typically, commodity contracts are reversed, or terminated, prior to their consummation. For instance, as the initial buyer of 1,000 bushels of corn, you may enter into a similar contract to sell the same quantity, thus in effect closing out your position.

Table 11.1 shows the unit size of certain commodity contracts.

Table 11.1 **Unit Size of Some Commodity Contracts**

Contract	Contract Stated In
Wheat	5,000 bu.
Cattle	40,000 lb.
Coffee	37,500 lb.
Cotton	50,000 lb.
Sugar	112,000 lb.

A person can invest directly in a commodity or indirectly through a mutual fund. A third method is to buy into a limited partnership involved in commodity investments. The mutual fund and partnership strategies are more conservative, since risk is spread and management know-how provided.

Investors may engage in commodity trading in the hope of high return rates and inflation hedges. In inflation, commodities move favorably since they are tied into economic trends. But high risk and uncertainty exist because commodity prices vacillate and because there is much low-margin investing. Investors must have plenty of cash available in the event of margin calls and to cover their losses. To reduce risk, commodities investors should hold a diversified portfolio, and they should determine the integrity and reliability of the sales person.

The buyer of a commodity always has the option of terminating the contract or letting it run to gain possible higher profits. On the other hand, he or she may utilize the earnings to put up margin on another futures contract. This is referred to as an *inverse pyramid* in a futures contract.

Commodity futures exchanges enable buyers and sellers to negotiate cash (spot) prices. Cash is paid for immediately receiving physical possession of a commodity. Prices in the cash market rely to some degree on prices in the futures market. In fact, cash prices for commodities are near prices in the short-term futures market. There may be higher prices for the commodity over time, incorporating holding costs and anticipated inflation.

Commodity and financial futures are traded in the Chicago Board of Trade, which is the largest exchange. Other exchanges exist, some specializing in given commodities. Examples of commodity exchanges are the New York Cotton Exchange, Chicago Mercantile Exchange, and Amex Commodities Exchange. Since there is a chance of significant gains and losses in commodities, exchanges have restrictions on the highest daily price movements for a commodity. Regulation of the commodities exchanges is by the federal Commodity Futures Trading Commission.

The financial pages of some newspapers, such as the *Wall Street Journal*, provide the beginning, high, low, and ending (settle) prices for each day, along with the daily change for the commodity. In addition, the all-time high and low are provided. *Open interest* is the number of outstanding futures contracts for the commodity and the expiration dates (see Figure 11.1).

Thursday, May 23, 1985.

Open Interest Reflects Previous Trading Day.

	Open	High	Low	Settle	Change	Lifetime High	Low	Open Interest
COTTON (CTN)—50,000 lbs.; cents per lb.								
July	65.32	65.32	64.55	64.62 −	.64	79.85	63.86	5,887
Oct	63.80	63.80	63.51	63.53 −	.20	77.50	63.51	1,555
Dec	63.75	63.78	63.50	63.60 −	.15	73.00	63.50	6,247
Mar86	64.76	64.76	64.44	64.56 −	.27	71.50	64.44	938
May	65.40	65.40	65.20	65.16 −	.27	70.00	65.20	292
July	65.70	65.70	65.45	65.45 −	.35	70.05	65.45	195
Est vol 2,200; vol Wed 1,150; open int 15,130, −105								
ORANGE JUICE (CTN)—15,000 lbs.; cents per lb.								
July	144.75	146.00	143.60	144.10 −	.90	184.80	143.60	2,488
Sept	143.60	144.00	142.00	143.00 −	.90	182.00	142.00	1,765
Nov	142.30	142.50	141.40	142.00 −	.20	181.00	141.40	833
Jan86	142.00	142.00	141.00	141.70 −	.50	180.00	141.00	375
Mar	142.25	142.25	142.25	141.70 −	.50	177.50	142.25	242
Est vol 450; vol Wed 564; open int 5,774, −92.								
SUGAR—WORLD (CSCE)—112,000 lbs.; cents per lb.								
July	3.02	3.10	2.96	3.07 +	.03	9.95	2.92	22,706
Sept	3.17	3.22	3.15	3.22 +	.01	9.75	3.06	1,279
Oct	3.32	3.40	3.26	3.39 +	.05	9.05	3.17	38,262
Jan86	3.76	3.76	3.76	3.81 +	.04	7.75	3.60	274
Mar	4.22	4.26	4.15	4.25 +	.01	8.27	3.98	19,021
May	4.38	4.44	4.35	4.43	....	7.15	4.20	5,103
July	4.58	4.62	4.56	4.63 +	.02	6.69	4.45	4,009
Oct	4.93	4.94	4.93	4.94 +	.02	4.94	4.70	161
Est vol 7,525; vol Wed 13,194; open int 90,836, −554.								

Source: *Wall Street Journal*, May 23, 1985.

Figure 11.1   Futures Prices

The return on a futures contract comes from *capital gain* (selling price minus purchase price) since no current income is involved. High capital gain is possible due to price volatility of the commodity and the effect of leverage from the low margin requirement. However, if things go sour, the entire investment in the form of margin could be lost quickly. The return on investment when dealing in commodities (whether a long or short position) equals:

$$\frac{\text{Selling price} - \text{purchase price}}{\text{Margin deposit}}$$

Let's say, for example, that you purchase a contract on a commodity for $60,000, putting up an initial deposit of $5,000. You later sell the contract for $64,000. The return is:

$$\frac{\$64,000 - \$60,000}{\$5,000} = 80\%$$

Margin requirements for commodity contracts are relatively low, usually ranging from 5% to 10% of the contract's value. (For stocks, you will remember, the margin requirement is 50% of the cost of the security.) In commodities trading, no money is really lent, and so no interest is paid.

An *initial margin* is required as a *deposit* on the futures contract. The purpose of the deposit is to cover a market value decline on the contract. The amount of the deposit depends on the nature of the contract and the commodity exchange involved.

Investors also have to put up a *maintenance deposit*, which is lower than the initial deposit and provides the minimum margin that must always be maintained in the account. It is usually about 80% of the initial margin.

Let's look at an example: On July 1, you enter into a contract to buy 37,500 pounds of coffee at $5 a pound to be delivered by October 1. The value of the total contract is $187,500. Assume the initial margin requirement is 10%, or $18,750. The margin maintenance requirement is 70%, or $13,125. If there is a contract loss of $1,500, you must put up the $1,500 to cover the margin position; otherwise, the contract will be terminated with the resulting loss.

As a second example, assume you make an initial deposit of $10,000 on a contract and a maintenance deposit of $7,500. If the market value of the contract does not decrease by more than $2,500, you'll have no problem. However, if the market value of the contract declines by $4,500, the margin on deposit will go to $5,500, and you will have to deposit another $5,500 in order to keep the sum at the initial deposit level. If you don't come up with the additional $5,500, the contract will be canceled.

Commodity trading may be in the form of hedging, speculating, or spreading.

Investors use *hedging* to protect their position in a commodity. For example, a citrus grower (the seller) will hedge to get a higher price for his products while a processor (or buyer) of the item will hedge to obtain a lower price. By hedging an investor minimizes the risk of loss but loses the prospect of sizable profit.

Now let's say that a commodity is currently selling at $120 a pound, but the potential buyer (assume a manufacturer) expects the price to rise in the future. To guard against higher prices, the buyer acquires a futures contract selling at $135 a pound. Six months later, the price of the commodity moves to $180. The futures contract price will similarly increase to, say, $210. The buyer's profit is $75 a pound. If 5,000 pounds are involved, the total profit is $375,000. At the same time, the cost on the market rose by only $60 a pound, or $300,000. In effect, the manufacturer has hedged his position, coming out with a profit of $75,000, and has kept the rising costs of the commodity under control.

Some people invest in commodities for *speculative* purposes. Suppose that you purchase an October futures contract for 37,500 pounds of coffee at $5 a pound. If the price rises to $5.40, you'll gain $.40 a pound for a total gain of $15,000. The percent gain, considering the initial margin requirement, is 80%. If the transactions occurred over a two-month period, your annual gain would be 480%. This resulted from a mere 7.4% gain in the price of a pound of coffee.

Spreading attempts to take advantage of wide swings in price and at the same time puts a cap on loss exposure. Spreading is similar to stock option trading. The investor enters into at least two contracts to obtain some profit while limiting loss potential. He or she purchases one contract and sells the other in the hope of achieving a minimal but reasonable profit. If the worst happens, the spread helps to minimize the investor's loss.

As an example, suppose you acquire Contract 1 for 10,000 pounds of commodity Z at $500 a pound. At the same time, you sell short Contract 2 for 10,000 pounds of the same commodity at $535 a pound. Subsequently, you sell Contract 1 for $520 a pound and buy Contract 2 for $543 a pound. Contract 1 yields a profit of $20 a pound while Contract 2 takes a loss of $8 a pound. On net, however, you earn a profit of $12 a pound, so your total gain is $120,000.

Financial Futures

The basic types of financial futures are: (1) interest rate futures; (2) foreign currency futures; and (3) stock-index futures. Financial futures trading is similar in many ways to commodity trading and now constitutes about two-thirds of all contracts. Because of the instability in interest and exchange rates, financial futures can be used to hedge. They can also be utilized as speculative investments because of the potential for significant price variability. Also financial futures have a lower margin requirement than commodities do. The margin on a U.S. Treasury bill, for example, may be as low as 2%.

Financial futures are traded in the New York Futures Exchange, Amex Commodities Exchange, International Monetary Market (part of Chicago Mercantile Exchange), and the Chicago Board of Trade. Primarily, financial futures are for fixed income debt securities to hedge or speculate on interest rate changes and foreign currency.

An *interest rate futures contract* provides the holder with the right to a given amount of the related debt security at a later date (usually no more than three years). They may be in Treasury bills and notes, certificates of deposit, commercial paper, and GNMA certificates, among others.

Interest rate futures are stated as a percentage of the par value of the applicable debt security. The value of interest rate futures contracts is directly tied into interest rates. For example, as interest rates decrease, the value of the contract increases. As the price or quote of the contract goes up, the purchaser of the contract has the gain while the seller loses. A change of one basis point in interest rates causes a price change. A basis point is 1/100 of 1%.

Those who trade in interest rate futures do not usually take possession of the financial instrument. In essence, the contract is used either to hedge or to speculate on future interest rates and security prices. For example, a banker might use interest rate futures to hedge his or her position.

As an example of hedging, assume a company will issue bonds in ninety days, and the underwriters are now working on the terms and conditions. Interest rates are expected to rise in the next three months. Thus, investors can hedge by selling short their Treasury bills. A rise in interest rates will result in a lower price to repurchase the interest rate future with the resulting profit. This will net against the increased interest cost of the debt issuance.

Speculators find financial futures attractive because of their potentially large return on a small investment. With large contracts (say, a $1,000,000 Treasury bill), even a small change in the price of the contract can provide significant gain. However, significant risk also exists with interest futures. They may involve volatile securities with great gain or loss potential. If you are a speculator hoping for increasing interest rates, you will want to sell an interest rate future, since it will soon decline in value.

A *currency futures contract* gives you a right to a specified amount of foreign currency at a future date. The contracts are standardized, and secondary markets do exist. Currency futures are expressed in dollars or cents per unit of the related foreign currency (see Figure 11.2). They typically have a delivery period of no more than one year. Table 11.2 provides trading units for some currencies.

Table 11.2   **Typical Currency Futures and Trading Units**

Currency	Trading Unit
British pound	25,000
Canadian dollar	100,000
Swiss franc	125,000
West German mark	125,000

Currency futures can be used for either hedging or speculation. The purpose of hedging in a currency is to lock into the best money exchange possible. Here's an example of hedging an exposed position: A manager enters into an agreement to get francs in four months. If the franc decreases compared to the dollar, the manager obtains less value. To hedge his exposure, the manager can sell a futures contract in francs by going short. If the franc

Thursday, May 23, 1985

The New York foreign exchange selling rates below apply to trading among banks in amounts of $1 million and more, as quoted at 3 p.m. Eastern time by Bankers Trust Co. Retail transactions provide fewer units of foreign currency per dollar.

Country	U.S. $ equiv. Thurs.	Wed.	Currency per U.S. $ Thurs.	Wed.
Argentina (Peso)	.001848	.002252	541.00	444.00
Australia (Dollar)	.6795	.6930	1.4716	1.4430
Austria (Schilling)	.04615	.04623	21.670	21.630
Belgium (Franc)				
Commercial rate	.01611	.01614	62.080	61.950
Financial rate	.01604	.01607	62.320	62.220
Brazil (Cruzeiro)	.0001880	.0002024	5320.00	4940.00
Britain (Pound)	1.2645	1.2560	.7908	.7962
30-Day Forward	1.2595	1.2510	.7939	.7994
90-Day Forward	1.2507	1.2415	.7996	.8055
180-Day Forward	1.2412	1.2320	.8057	.8117
Canada (Dollar)	.7291	.7302	1.3715	1.3694
30-Day Forward	.7281	.7294	1.3735	1.3710
90-Day Forward	.7263	.7277	1.3768	1.3742
180-Day Forward	.7241	.7255	1.3810	1.3784
Chile (Official rate)	.006579	.006674	152.00	149.84
China (Yuan)	.3532	.3532	2.8309	2.8309
Colombia (Peso)	.007305	.007560	136.90	132.27
Denmark (Krone)	.09025	.09046	11.0800	11.0550
Ecuador (Sucre)				
Official rate	.01489	.01489	67.18	67.18
Floating rate	.009091	.008849	110.00	113.00
Finland (Markka)	.1559	.1563	6.4150	6.4000
France (Franc)	.1064	.1064	9.4000	9.4000
30-Day Forward	.1062	.1062	9.4180	9.4180
90-Day Forward	.1058	.1058	9.4480	9.4480
180-Day Forward	.1054	.1054	9.4870	9.4900
Greece (Drachma)	.007353	.007396	136.00	135.20
Hong Kong (Dollar)	.1287	.1287	7.7720	7.7725
India (Rupee)	.08032	.08065	12.45	12.40
Indonesia (Rupiah)	.0008969	.00090	1115.00	1111.00
Ireland (Punt)	1.0160	1.0190	.9843	.9814
Israel (Shekel)	.0009901	.0001050	1010.00	952.03
Italy (Lira)	.0005081	.0005094	1968.00	1963.00
Japan (Yen)	.003980	.003985	251.25	250.95
30-Day Forward	.003985	.003990	250.91	250.61
90-Day Forward	.003998	.004001	250.15	249.92
180-Day Forward	.004019	.004023	248.80	248.58
Lebanon (Pound)	.06135	.05755	16.30	17.375
Malaysia (Ringgit)	.4047	.4062	2.4710	2.4620
Mexico (Peso)				
Floating rate	.003984	.004016	251.00	249.00
Netherlands (Guilder)	.2878	.2886	3.4750	3.4650
New Zealand (Dollar)	.4520	.4535	2.2123	2.2051
Norway (Krone)	.1126	.1128	8.8800	8.8625
Pakistan (Rupee)	.06329	.06337	15.80	15.78
Peru (Sol)	.0001026	.0001104	9747.00	9056.59
Philippines (Peso)	.05568	.05408	17.96	18.49
Portugal (Escudo)	.005763	.005797	173.50	172.50
Saudi Arabia (Riyal)	.2771	.2771	3.6090	3.6090

Source: *Wall Street Journal*, May 23, 1985.

Figure 11.2   *Foreign Exchange*

declines in value, the futures contract will make a profit, thus offsetting the manager's loss when he receives the francs.

As an example of speculation, assume a standardized contract of 100,000 pounds. In February you buy a currency futures contract for delivery in June. The contract price is $1 equals 2 pounds. The total value of the contract is $50,000, and the margin requirement is $6,000. The pound strengthens until it equals 1.8 pounds to $1. Hence, the value of your contract increases to $55,556, giving you a return of 92.6%. If the pound had weakened, you would have taken a loss on the contract.

A *stock-index futures contract* is tied into a broad stock market index. Introduced in 1982, futures contracts at the present time can apply to the S & P 500 Stock Index, New York Stock Exchange Composite Stock Index, and Value Line Composite Stock Index. However, smaller investors can avail themselves of the S & P 100 futures contract which involves a smaller margin deposit. Stock-index futures allow you to participate in the general change in the entire stock market. You can buy and sell the "market as a whole" rather than a specific security. If you anticipate a bull market but are unsure which particular stock will rise, you should buy (long position) a stock-index future. Because of the risks involved, you should trade in stock-index futures *only* for the purpose of hedging or speculation.

Review

1. What is a futures contract?

   an agreement for delivery of a commodity, financial instrument, or currency at a specified price by a certain date

2. What terms are specified in a futures contract?

   the amount, quality, valuation method, delivery means, month of delivery, and exchange to be traded on

3. (T,F) The futures market consists of commodities only.

   False

4. A contract to deliver a Treasury note is a _____ future.

   financial

5. The long position means _____ a contract in hope of a price rise.

   buying

6. You take a short position when you _____ a contract.

sell

7. (T,F) To close a position, the purchaser of a contract may sell a similar one.

True

8. (T,F) Buyers of futures contracts usually take physical possession of the item.

False

9. (T,F) Commissions on futures vary in amount.

True

10. (T,F) A security brokerage account is sufficient to trade in commodities.

False

11. (T,F) Futures contracts may be a good inflation hedge.

True

12. (T,F) Futures commodity contract prices are very stable.

False

13. Prices of commodities are influenced by _____.

many variables including political, economic, and environmental conditions

14. (T,F) Futures contracts are usually valid for no more than one year.

True

15. (T,F) Futures contracts are on a margin basis.

True

16. (T,F) One can invest in a commodity indirectly through a mutual fund.

True

17. **(T,F)** Significant gain can occur with a futures contract because of price volatility and the effect of leverage from the low margin requirement.

True

18. The largest exchange for commodities is the _____.

Chicago Board of Trade

19. The closing price of a commodity for a particular day is referred to as the _____ price.

ending or settle

20. What is daily trading limit?

the limit on the maximum daily price change for a commodity contract

21. What is open interest?

the number of outstanding futures contracts for the commodity and the expiration date

22. What is an inverse pyramid in futures contracts?

use of the gain derived from one contract to provide a margin for other futures contracts

23. **(T,F)** The sole source of return from a commodity future is capital gain.

True

24. The margin for commodity contracts usually does not exceed _____%.

10

25. You purchase a contract for 10,000 pounds of a commodity at $.30 a pound and sell it for $.46 a pound. The initial deposit is $500. What is the percentage of return on your investment?

$$\frac{\text{Profit}}{\text{Investment}} = \frac{\$.16 \times 10,000}{\$500} = \frac{\$1,600}{\$500} = 320\%$$

26. What is a maintenance deposit?

It is lower than the initial margin and provides the minimum amount of margin to be retained in the account.

27. **(T,F)** Interest is not paid on a margined commodity contract.

True

28. On a commodity contract, the margin requirement is $5,000 and the maintenance margin is 70%. How much can price decline before additional margin must be put up?

Initial margin	$5,000
Minus maintenance margin (70% × $5,000)	3,500
Maximum loss	$1,500

29. You buy a contract for 10,000 pounds of commodity A at $4.00 a pound, putting up an initial margin of 10%. If the price increases to $4.20 a pound in three months, what is the percentage gain and what is the annual gain?

$$\text{Percentage gain} = \frac{\$.20 \times 10,000 \text{ lbs.}}{10\% \times \$40,000} = \frac{\$2,000}{\$4,000} = 50\%$$

Annual gain = 50% × 4 = 200%

30. What is spreading?

---

combining two or more contracts into one position to obtain the advantage of fluctuating prices at the same time limiting loss potential

31. How is the options market different from the commodities futures market?

An investor in the options market has a limited loss up to the purchase price paid. No additional funds have to be put up. In the commodities futures market, however, an initial margin on a contract may be gone in the first day, requiring the investor to put up additional funds.

32. What do the options market and commodities futures market have in common?

They both have high trading volume with minimal delivery of actual items between buyer and seller.

33. What is a financial future?

an agreement to buy or sell a given amount of a certain financial instrument at a specified price at a predetermined date

34. (T,F) Most interest rate futures have an expiration period of no more than three months.

False

35. How are interest rate futures stated?

as a percentage of the par value of the related debt security

36. (T,F) When interest rates increase, the value of a financial futures contract decreases.

True

37. (T,F) A foreign currency futures contract provides the investor with the right to a given amount of foreign currency at a later date.

True

38. (T,F) Secondary markets do exist for currency futures contracts.

True

39. You purchase a currency futures contract for 100,000 pounds for delivery in September when $1 equals 2.2 pounds; the margin requirement is $9,000. In September, the exchange rate has changed so that $1 now equals 1.7 pounds.
   a. What was the total value of the contract when you bought it?
   b. What is the total value of the contract in September?
   c. What is the rate of return based on the cash paid?

a. $\dfrac{100{,}000 \text{ pounds}}{2.2} = \$45{,}455$

b. $\dfrac{100{,}000 \text{ pounds}}{1.7} = \$58{,}824$

c. $\dfrac{\$13{,}369}{\$9{,}000} = 148.5\%$

40. A _____ contract relates to the change in a general stock-market index such as the S & P 500 Stock Index. If a bear market is anticipated, you should _____ the futures contract.

stock-index futures, sell short

Self-Test

1. Futures contracts can be for _____ and _____.
2. When a futures contract is sold, it is said to be in a _____ position.
3. **(T,F)** A commodities trader needs only a security brokerage account.
4. Commodity contracts usually last no more than _____.
5. **(T,F)** Futures contracts cannot be on margin.
6. Which of the following is a good reason to invest in commodity contracts?
   a. low risk
   b. tax free
   c. annual income
   d. leverage
7. The largest exchange for futures trading is:
   a. New York Stock Exchange
   b. Amex
   c. Chicago Board of Trade
   d. over-the-counter
8. The ending price of a commodity for the day is called the _____ price.
9. The _____ regulates commodities exchanges.
10. The number of outstanding futures contracts for a commodity along with the expiration date is referred to as the _____.
11. Using the profit obtained from one contract to furnish the margin for other futures contracts is called the _____.
12. The return on futures contracts is in the form of _____.
13. Margin requirements for commodities typically range from
    a. 2% to 5%
    b. 20% to 30%

  c. 5% to 10%
  d. 50% to 60%

14. You buy a contract for 10,000 pounds of a commodity at $.50 a pound and sell it for $.62 a pound. Your initial deposit is $400. What percentage return do you earn?

15. What is a maintenance deposit?

16. On a commodity contract, the margin requirement is $6,000 and the maintenance margin is 80%. How much can price decrease before further margin must be given?

17. What is spreading?

18. An interest futures contract may be taken on all of the following except:
  a. certificate of deposit
  b. commercial paper
  c. Treasury bill
  d. stock

19. Interest rate futures are stated as a percentage of _____ of the related debt security.

20. The value of a financial futures contract _____ as interest rates decrease.

21. A one basis point in interest rates equals _____ of 1%.

22. The margin requirement on a financial futures contract is _____ than on a commodities futures contract.

23. (T,F) No secondary market exists for currency futures contracts.

24. You buy a currency futures contract of 100,000 pounds for delivery in November when $1 equals 2.4 pounds. The margin required is $8,000. In November, the exchange rate is $1 equals 1.8 pounds.
  a. What is the total value of the contract when purchased?
  b. What is the total value of the contract in November?
  c. What rate of return do you earn on your cash investment?

25. In which broad stock indexes can a stock-index futures contract be transacted?

26. (T,F) If a bull market is anticipated, you should buy (long position) a stock-index futures contract.

Self-Test Answers

1. commodities, financial instruments
2. short
3. False
4. one year
5. False
6. d
7. c
8. ending or settle
9. Commodity Futures Trading Commission
10. open interest

11. inverse pyramid
12. capital gain
13. c

14. $\dfrac{\text{Profit}}{\text{Investment}} = \dfrac{\$.12 \times 10,000}{\$400} = \dfrac{\$1,200}{\$400} = 300\%$

15. It is less than the initial deposit and represents the minimum margin that has to be kept in the account.

16.

Initial margin	$6,000
Minus maintenance margin (80% × $6,000)	−4,800
Maximum loss	$1,200

17. Spreading capitalizes on significant variability in price at the same time placing a ceiling on loss exposure. Two or more contracts are made to achieve a desired return. For example, one contract may be bought and the other sold.

18. d
19. par value
20. increases
21. 1/100
22. lower
23. False

24. **a.** $\dfrac{100,000 \text{ lbs.}}{2.4} = \$41,667$

   b. $\dfrac{100,000 \text{ lbs.}}{1.8} = \$55,556$

   c. $\dfrac{\$13,888}{\$\ 8,000} = 173.6\%$

25. S & P 500 Stock Index
New York Stock Exchange Composite Stock Index
Value Line Composite Stock Index

26. True

PORTFOLIO ANALYSIS AND MANAGEMENT

12

Objectives

When you complete this chapter, you will be able to:

- Define portfolio return and risk
- Discuss the capital asset pricing model (CAPM)
- Understand the security market line (SML)
- Read mutual fund quotations
- Identify the types of portfolio funds
- Rate and measure the performance of mutual funds

Most financial assets are held as part of a portfolio. Therefore, the risk-return analysis discussed in Chapter 3 should not be confined to single assets only. As an investor, you must be able to anticipate return and risk on the portfolio as a whole, not just on one asset.

Portfolio Return and Risk

The expected return on a portfolio (r_p) is simply the weighted average return of the individual securities in the portfolio, the weights being the fraction of the total funds invested in each asset:

$$r_p = w_1 r_1 + w_2 r_2 + \ldots + w_n r_n$$

$$= \sum_{j=1}^{n} w_j r_j$$

where the r_j's are the expected returns in individual securities; the w's are the fractions; n is the number of assets in the portfolio; and

$$\sum_{j=1}^{n} w_j = 1.0.$$

Unlike returns, the risk of a portfolio (σ_p) is not simply a weighted average of the standard deviations of the individual securities in the portfolio. In a two-asset portfolio, the portfolio risk is defined as

$$\sigma_p = \sqrt{w_A^2 \sigma_A^2 + w_B^2 \sigma_B^2 + 2 w_A w_B P_{AB} \sigma_A \sigma_B}$$

where σ_A and σ_B are the standard deviations of the possible returns from security A and security B.

w_A and w_B are the weights of fractions of total funds invested in security A and security B, and P_{AB} is the correlation coefficient between security A and security B. By the way, the correlation coefficient is the measurement of joint movement between two securities.

Diversification

As can be seen in the previous formula, the portfolio risk, measured in terms of σ_p, is not the weighted average of the individual asset risks in the portfolio. We have in the formula of σ_p the third term—$2 w_A w_B P_{AB} \sigma_A \sigma_B$—which makes a significant contribution to the overall portfolio risk. This formula shows that the portfolio risk can be minimized or completely eliminated by *diversification*. The degree of reduction in portfolio risk depends on the correlation between the assets being combined. Generally speaking, by combining two perfectly negatively correlated assets ($P_{AB} = -1.0$), we are able to eliminate the risk completely. In the real world, however, most securities are negatively but not perfectly correlated. In fact, most assets are positively correlated. We could still reduce the portfolio risk by combining even positively correlated assets.

Markowitz's Efficient Portfolio

Dr. Harry Markowitz in the early 1950s provided a theoretical framework for the systematic composition of optimum portfolios. Using a technique called *quadratic programming*, he attempted to select from among hundreds of individual securities, given certain basic information supplied by portfolio

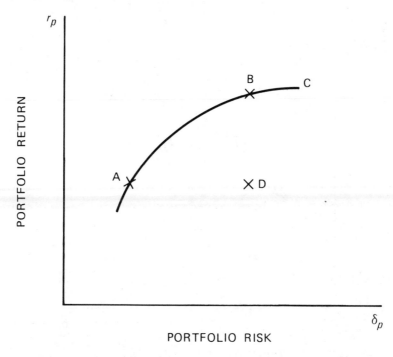

Figure 12.1 *Efficient Portfolio*

managers and security analysts. He also weighted these selections in compos-
ing portfolios. Much of the Markowitz portfolio model is beyond the scope of
this book. Only the general idea behind the model is presented here.

The central theme of Markowitz's work is that rational investors behave in
a way that reflects their aversion to taking increased risk without being compensated by an adequate increase in expected return. Also, for any given expected return, most investors will prefer a lower risk, and for any given level
of risk, they will prefer a higher return to a lower return. Markowitz showed
how quadratic programming could be used to calculate a set of "efficient" portfolios such as those illustrated by the curve in Figure 12.1 and Figure 12.2. These
diagrams reflect an efficient set of portfolios that lie along the ABC line, called
the *efficient frontier*. Along this frontier, the investor can receive a maximum
return for a given level of risk or a minimum risk for a given level of return.
If we compare portfolios A, B, and D, we see that A and B are clearly more
efficient than D. Portfolio A could produce the same expected return but at
a lower risk level, while B would have the same degree or risk as D but would
afford a higher return.

To see how the investor tries to find the optimum portfolio, we first introduce
the *indifference curve*, which shows the investor's trade-off between risk and
return. Figure 12.3 shows the indifference curves for two investors. The steeper
the curve, the more averse to risk the investor is. For example, investor B's
curve is steeper than investor A's. This means that investor B will want more
incremental return for each additional unit of risk. Figure 12.4 depicts a fami-

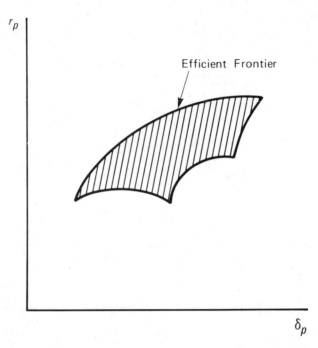

Figure 12.2 *Efficient Frontier*

ly of indifference curves for investor A. The objective is to maximize the investor's satisfaction by attaining the highest curve possible.

By matching the indifference curve showing the risk-return trade-off with the best investments available in the market as represented by points on the efficient frontier, investors are able to find an optimum portfolio. According to Markowitz, investor A will achieve the highest possible curve at point B along the efficient frontier. Point B is thus the optimum portfolio for this investor.

The Market Index Model

For even a moderate-size portfolio, the formulas for portfolio return and risk require estimation of a large number of input data. Concerned with the computational burden in deriving these estimates led to the development of the following *market index model*:

$$r_j = a + br_m$$

where r_j = return on security j; r_m = return on the market portfolio; and b = the beta or systematic risk of a security (see Chapter 3).

This model attempts to measure the systematic or uncontrollable risk of a security. The beta is measured as follows:

$$b = \frac{\text{cov}(r_j, r_m)}{\sigma_m^2}$$

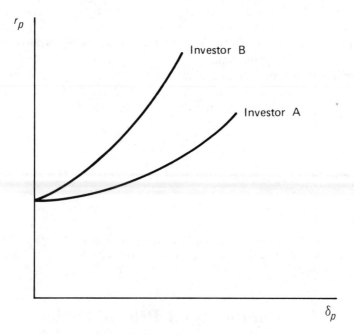

Figure 12.3 *Risk-Return Indifference Curves*

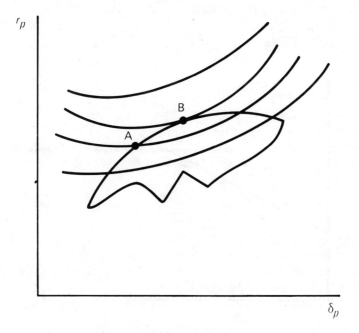

Figure 12.4 *Matching the Efficient Frontier and Indifference Curves*

where $Cov(r_j,r_m)$ = the covariance of the returns of the securities with the market return, and σ_m^2 = the variance (standard deviation squared) of the market return. (The market return is the return on the Standard and Poor's 500 or Dow Jones 30 Industrials.)

An easier way to compute beta is to determine the slope of the "least-squares" linear regression line $(r_j - r_f)$, where the excess return of the security $(r_j - r_f)$ is regressed against the excess return of the market portfolio $(r_m - r_f)$. The formula for beta is:

$$ b = \frac{\Sigma MK - n\overline{M}\overline{K}}{(\Sigma M^2 - n\overline{M^2})} $$

where $M = (r_m - r_f)$; $K = (r_j - r_f)$; n = the number of periods; $\overline{M}$= the average of M; and $\overline{K}$ = the average of K.

The market index model was initially proposed to reduce the number of data required in portfolio analysis. It can also be justified in the context of the *capital asset pricing model*.

The Capital Asset Pricing Model

The capital asset pricing model (CAPM) takes off where the efficient frontier concluded, with an assumption that there exists a risk-free security with a single rate that investors can borrow and lend at. By combining the risk-free asset and the efficient frontier, we create a whole new set of investment opportunities that will allow us to reach higher indifference curves than would be possible simply along the efficient frontier. The $r_f mx$ line in Figure 12.5 shows this possibility. This line is called the capital market line (CML), and the formula for this line is:

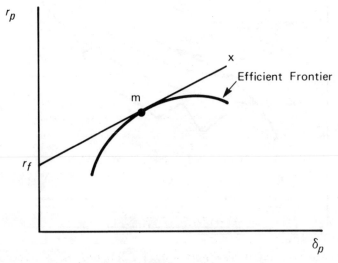

Figure 12.5   *Graph of CAPM*

$$r_p = r_f + \left(\frac{r_m - r_f}{\sigma_m - 0} \right) \sigma_p$$

which indicates that the expected return on any portfolio (r_p) is equal to the risk-free return (r_f) plus the slope of the line times a value along the horizontal axis (σ_p), indicating the amount of risk undertaken.

The Security Market Line

We can establish the trade-off between risk and return for an individual security through the security market line (SML) shown in Figure 12.6. Here SML is a general relationship to show the risk-return trade-off for an individual security whereas CML achieves the same objective for a portfolio. The formula for SML is:

$$r_j = r_f + b(r_m - r_f)$$

This formula was introduced in Chapter 3. The model shows that investors in individual securities are assumed to be rewarded only for systematic, uncontrollable, market-related risk, known as the beta (b) risk. All other risk is assumed to be diversified away and thus is not rewarded.

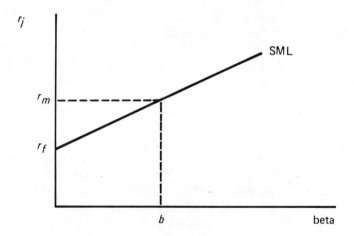

Figure 12.6   *The Security Market Line (SML)*

Mutual Funds

Mutual funds are popular investment vehicles that represent ownership in a professionally managed portfolio of securities that are actively traded. The investor receives shares of stock in the mutual fund. The major advantage of investing in mutual funds is *diversification*. Another advantage is that the mutual fund is a portfolio that is professionally managed. Also, investors can own a variety of securities with a minimal capital investment. Further, there may exist dividend reinvestment and check-writing options. Mutual funds are also convenient because all recordkeeping is done by the fund. There are some drawbacks, however. Mutual funds are costly to acquire because of sizable commissions and professional management fees. Traditionally, mutual fund performance has not significantly outperformed the market as a whole.

Quotations for mutual funds are fairly straightforward and are stated in dollars and cents. Here is a quote for Kemper Funds—Growth, published on December 27, 1984:

	NAV	Offer Price	NAV Chg.
Kemper Funds Growth	11.22	12.26	+.02

The quotation tells us that on December 26, 1984, a share in the fund could be sold for $11.22—the NAV, or net asset value. On the same date, a share could be purchased for $12.26. The rather large difference between the sale price and the purchase price is due to the commission charged on the purchase transaction. The NAV Chg. value of +.02 indicates that the sale price (NAV) increased by 2 cents a share from the preceding day.

Mutual funds may be classified into different types, according to organization, the fees charged, methods of trading funds, and their investment objectives. In open-end funds, investors buy from and sell their shares back to the fund itself. Closed-end funds operate with a fixed number of shares outstanding. These shares are traded like common stocks among individuals in secondary markets. All open- and closed-end funds charge management fees and are called *load funds*. *No-load funds* do not charge fees.

Mutual funds can be specialized; for example, you can have gold funds, tax-free bond funds, or money market funds. These funds have different investment objectives: growth, safety and income, capital appreciation, growth plus income, etc. If you are interested in investing in mutual funds you should study the funds' prospectus in order to select one that meets your investment goals.

Investors turn to *index* funds to control portfolio risk and/or guarantee market performance. An index fund is a portfolio designed to mirror the movement of a selected broad market index (such as Standard and Poor's 500) by holding investment commitments in the same proportions as those that comprise the index itself. An index fund by definition has a beta of 1.0.

A description of some of the different types of mutual funds follows.

With a *growth fund*, the objective is capital appreciation, so investment is made in common stocks evidencing growth possibilities. Thus, securities providing current income in the form of dividends and interest income are avoided. A disadvantage, however, is that growth funds entail greater investment risk. Aggressive investors are attracted to growth funds.

Income funds are designed to furnish current income in the form of dividend and interest income. Capital gain is *not* the objective. The portfolio primarily consists of high dividend common stock, preferred stock, and debt securities. High-quality securities are typically purchased. Investors looking for attractive returns favor these funds.

Balanced funds generate capital gains and current income. A high percentage investment is made in high-quality common stock to obtain capital gain, and about one-fourth of the portfolio is in stable fixed-income securities to obtain current income. There is typically a safe return with a minimal amount of risk undertaken. In essence, balanced funds are a hybrid between growth and income funds.

Bond funds invest in varying types and grades of bonds. The prime emphasis is on receiving interest income. These funds generally offer liquidity, safety, and diversification. However, bond prices are significantly affected by changing interest rates. Some bond funds invest only in municipal bonds to obtain tax-free income, which is beneficial to investors in high tax brackets.

Money market funds invest in short-term money market securities such as commercial paper and certificates of deposit. These funds offer liquidity and low risk. The return on a money market fund typically exceeds the return earned on a bank account.

Certain other funds emphasize investment in one industry or in a group of related industries. The major purpose of such funds is to generate an attractive rate of return. However, high risk is typically involved. Also, specialized knowledge of the industry is required.

Generally, mutual funds provide returns to investors in the form of: (1) dividend income; (2) capital gains distribution; and (3) change in capital or net asset value (NAV) of the fund. The holding period return (HPR) for mutual funds is basically the same as that for stocks. Specifically, HPR equals investment income dividends plus capital gains distributions plus ending-NAV-minus-beginning-NAV, divided by beginning NAV.

Care must be taken in computing HPR to differentiate between before-tax HPR and after-tax HPR. Of course, after-tax HPR is the accurate measure of return.

Each year the August 15 issue of *Forbes* publishes a list of mutual funds and their average returns over a 10- to 15-year period, as well as in the last 12 months. Also, in assessing fund performance, investors must resort to the published beta of the funds being considered, because beta is a measure of risk relative to the market portfolio, such as Standard and Poor's 500 or Dow Jones 30 Industrials.

Review

1. Most financial assets are not held as part of a _____.

---

portfolio

2. What is portfolio return?

___

The portfolio return is the expected return on a portfolio, computed as the weighted average return of the individual securities in the portfolio, the weights being the fraction of the total funds invested in each security.

3. **(T,F)** Portfolio risk is a weighted average of the standard deviations of the individual securities in the portfolio.

___

False

4. Effective diversification results when returns on various securities are _____ correlated with each other.

___

negatively

5. On the efficient frontier, the investor can receive a maximum return for a given level of risk or a _____ for a given level of return.

___

minimum risk

6. To find the optimum portfolio, an investor can make use of the _____ curve.

___

indifference

7. Beta is an index of _____.

___

systematic (noncontrollable, nondiversifiable) risk

8. **(T,F)** The efficient portfolio having the lowest risk should also have the lowest expected return.

___

False

9. A portfolio on the efficient frontier that is tangent to the investor's indifference curve is called a(n) _____ portfolio.

___

optimum

10. The part of the price change for a stock or a portfolio that is due to changes in prices of the market as a whole is called

    a. systematic risk
    b. diversifiable risk
    c. standard deviation
    d. none of the above

    a

11. The _____ shows the risk and return levels for portfolios.

    capital market line

12. (T,F) A graph of the CAPM model is called the yield curve.

    False

13. The _____ shows that the required rate of return on a security is equal to the risk-free rate plus risk premium.

    security line or **CAPM** model

14. _____ is the difference between the risk-free rate and the expected return on the market portfolio.

    Risk premium

15. The standard used in defining the risk-free rate is the return available on _____.

    U.S. Treasury bills

16. (T,F) The proxy for the market return is Dow Jones 30 Industrials or Moody's.

    False

17. The risk-free rate is 5%, and the expected return on the market portfolio is 13%. On the basis of the CAPM:
    a. What is the risk premium on the market?
    b. What is the required rate of return on a security with a beta equal to 1.2?
    c. If the market expects a return of 12.5% from a stock, what is its beta?

    a. risk premium $= (r_m - r_f) = 13\% - 5\% - 8\%$

b. $r_j = r_f + b(r_m - r_f) = 5\% + 1.2(13\% - 5\%) = 5\% + 9.6\% = 14.6\%$

c. $12.5\% = 5\% + b(13\% - 5\%)$. Solving for beta gives $b = 1.25$.

18. If Treasury bills yield 10% and Alpha Company's expected return for the next year is 18% and its beta is 2, what is the market's return for the next year?

$18\% = 10\% + 2(r_m - 10\%)$. Solving for r_m gives 14%.

19. Assume the following:
The risk-free rate is 8%
The market portfolio return is 12%

Portfolio	Beta
A	.6
B	1.0
C	1.4

Calculate for each of the three portfolios the expected rate of return consistent with the CAPM Model.

Portfolio A $8\% + .6(12\% - 8\%) = 10.4\%$
Portfolio B $8\% + 1.0(12\% - 8\%) = 12.0\%$
Portfolio C $8\% + 1.4(12\% - 8\%) = 13.6\%$

20. Putting more of a portfolio into common stocks and less into bonds is likely to have:
   a. no change in either risk or return
   b. less risk, less return
   c. more return, less risk
   d. more risk, more return

   d

21. A group of stocks selected to behave the same as a broad market index and have a similar distribution of stocks is called a(n) _____.

   index fund

22. List a disadvantage of mutual fund ownership.

   sizable fees and management commissions

23. **(T,F)** In closed-end funds, investors buy from and sell their shares back to the fund itself.

_____

False

24. **(T,F)** Load funds do not charge management fees.

_____

False

25. List some types of mutual funds.

_____

growth funds, income funds, bond funds, money market funds

Self-Test

1. The _____ is the measurement of joint movement between two securities.
2. Dr. Markowitz provided a theoretical framework for the systematic composition of _____.
3. The use of the _____ was suggested as a way of getting around the problem of the excessive computational burden of the original Markowitz model.
4. _____ represents the portion of a security's risk that can be diversified away.
5. **(T,F)** Beta is an index of controllable risk.
6. Because any intelligent investor can eliminate risk by holding a diversified portfolio of securities, the appropriate measure of risk is
   a. correlation coefficient
   b. variance of the stock price
   c. beta
   d. covariance of the portfolio
7. When the market goes down, the best portfolio to own is the one with a beta of
   a. 0
   b. +0.5
   c. +1.5
   d. −2.0
8. When the market is expected to go up, the stock with the most promising profit potential would be the one with a beta of
   a. +1.5
   b. +1.0
   c. −1.0
   d. −0.5

9. The term "risk-free rate" implies a rate of return whereby the
    a. level of return does not vary over time
    b. underlying investment earning the return has a beta of 1
    c. expected rate of return equals the actual rate of return
    d. all of the above
10. **(T,F)** The risk premium is the additional return above that which could be earned on T-bills to compensate investors for assuming a given level of risk.

Self-Test Answers

1. correlation coefficient
2. optimum portfolios
3. market index model
4. Beta, or unsystematic risk
5. False
6. c
7. d
8. a
9. c
10. True

Appendix A

INVESTING WITH PERSONAL COMPUTERS

The use of microcomputers greatly aids the investing process by providing business and financial data immediately and enabling one to analyze the data quickly with predetermined criteria. A rating can be computed for all stocks or funds in the file.

Software exists to keep records of the investment portfolio, plot prices, and perform fundamental and technical analysis. Investment information can be accumulated in terms of shares, cost, dividends and/or interest income, and market price. Portfolio programs even assist in the timing of buy or sell decisions. Software also exists to spot the tax ramifications of a particular investment choice.

Through the use of communications software and modems, investors can obtain information from many on-line databases. Current prices and share-volume data may be obtained from such sources as Dow Jones and CompuServe. Investment advisory service analysis and recommendations are also available, including Standard and Poor's.

You can even buy and sell stocks through your personal computer. Brokers can be accessed through your system. Furthermore, computerized stock bulletin board services exist.

Spreadsheet Link

The *Dow Jones Spreadsheet Link* obtains financial data such as stock prices from Dow Jones News/Retrieval and puts them on a data disk. The data are then transferred to a spreadsheet where financial analysis calculations are made. Spreadsheet Link can be used with electronic worksheet programs from Lotus 1-2-3, VisiCalc, and MultiPlan.

Investment Analysis Software

Dow Jones Market Analyzer uses information from Dow Jones News/Retrieval to construct price and volume charts of securities, moving averages, and support and resistance lines. It performs a total of seventeen complex analyses.

Dow Jones Market Manager accesses Dow Jones News/Retrieval and enables the instant valuation of a portfolio. A *Tax Lot* accounting system records all transactions and assists in matching sell transactions with existing positions to minimize the tax liability applicable to capital gains and losses.

Dow Jones Market Microscope uses fundamental analysis techniques. It obtains fundamental data from Media General Financial Services and Corporate Earnings Estimator available from Dow Jones News/Retrieval. By establishing financial indicators, users can employ the data to generate screening reports and warnings. The program identifies securities meeting criteria standards and improves the timing of buys and sells.

Dow Jones Investment Evaluator is a basic portfolio management product. It permits the user to formulate multiple portfolios comprising stocks, bonds, mutual funds, options, and other securities. For more details on these programs, call 1-800-345-8500, extension 325.

Summa Software (503 644-3212) has the *Complete System*, which consists of the *Trader's Data Analyzer*, the *Trader's Forecaster*, and the *Trader's Accountant*. Summa's *Winning on Wall Street* permits the user to maintain a database of securities, perform technical analysis, and keep track of the investment portfolio. It generates charts and graphs allowing for technical analysis to properly time buys and sells. It shows the points where a stock price exceeds or goes below price trend lines.

The other investment-related software programs are too numerous to cover here. A detailed listing of investment management and financial analysis software appears in the March 1984 issue of *Interface Age*. New software is advertised and evaluated in *PC World's Annual Software Survey, Interface Age, Datamation*, and other magazines.

Someday a PC will allow the investor to monitor the ticker on all major exchanges, call up constant updates in relevant stocks, find out immediately when a stock passes a certain limit, and monitor the Dow Jones News Wire, all by using a single phone line. This technology is not here yet, but look for it in the future. The hardware exists today.

Appendix B

SELECTED INVESTMENT PUBLICATIONS

General Investment Sources

Publication	Publisher
American Stock Exchange Weekly Bulletin *(weekly)*	American Stock Exchange 86 Trinity Place New York, NY 10006
Babson's Investment and Barometer Letter *(weekly)*	Babson's Reports, Inc. Wellesley, MA 02181
Business Week *(weekly)*	McGraw-Hill 1221 Avenue of Americas New York, NY 10020
Commodity Service *(weekly)*	Dunn and Hargitt 22 North 2nd Street Lafayette, IN 47902
Dow Theory Forecasts *(weekly)*	Dow Theory Forecasts, Inc. 7412 Calumet Avenue Hammond, IN 46325
The Economist *(weekly)*	Economist Newspaper Ltd. 25 St. James's Strcct London, England

Forbes *(fortnightly)*   Forbes
                                        60 Fifth Avenue
                                        New York, NY 10011

The Kiplinger   Kiplinger Washington Editors
Washington Letter   1729 H Street, N.W.
(weekly)   Washington, DC 20006

New York Stock   New York Stock Exchange
Exchange Monthly   11 Wall Street
Review *(monthly)*   New York, NY 10005

Real Estate Investing   Harcourt Brace Jovanovich
Letter *(monthly)*   757 Third Avenue
                                        New York, NY 10017

Value Line Investment   Arnold Bernhard & Co.
Survey *(weekly)*   5 East 44th Street
                                        New York, NY 10017

Weekly Insider Report   Stock Research Corp.
(weekly)   55 Liberty Street
                                        New York, NY 10005

Professional Investment-Related Journals

Publication   *Publisher*

CFA Digest *(quarterly)*   Institute of Chartered Financial Analysts
                                        P.O. Box 3668
                                        Charlottesville, VA 22903

Commodity Journal   American Association of Commodity
(bimonthly)   Traders
                                        10 Park Street
                                        Concord, NH 03301

Financial Analysis Journal   Financial Analysts Federation
(bimonthly)   219 East 42nd Street
                                        New York, NY 10017

Institutional Investor   Institutional Investor Systems
(monthly)   488 Madison Avenue
                                        New York, NY 10022

Money Manager   Bond Buyer
(weekly)   One State Street Plaza
                                        New York, NY 10004

Wall Street Transcript   Wall Street Transcript
(weekly)   120 Wall Street
                                        New York, NY 10005

Appendix C

FUTURE VALUE AND PRESENT VALUE TABLES

Table 1 **Future Value of $1.00**

$$a_{\overline{n}|i} = (1 + i)^n$$

(n) Periods	2%	2½%	3%	4%	5%	6%
1	1.02000	1.02500	1.03000	1.04000	1.05000	1.06000
2	1.04040	1.05063	1.06090	1.08160	1.10250	1.12360
3	1.06121	1.07689	1.09273	1.12486	1.15763	1.19102
4	1.08243	1.10381	1.12551	1.16986	1.21551	1.26248
5	1.10408	1.13141	1.15927	1.21665	1.27628	1.33823
6	1.12616	1.15969	1.19405	1.26532	1.34010	1.41852
7	1.14869	1.18869	1.22987	1.31593	1.40710	1.50363
8	1.17166	1.21840	1.26677	1.36857	1.47746	1.59385
9	1.19509	1.24886	1.30477	1.42331	1.55133	1.68948
10	1.21899	1.28008	1.34392	1.48024	1.62889	1.79085
11	1.24337	1.31209	1.38423	1.53945	1.71034	1.89830
12	1.26824	1.34489	1.42576	1.60103	1.79586	2.01220
13	1.29361	1.37851	1.46853	1.66507	1.88565	2.13293
14	1.31948	1.41297	1.51259	1.73168	1.97993	2.26090
15	1.34587	1.44830	1.55797	1.80094	2.07893	2.39656
16	1.37279	1.48451	1.60471	1.87298	2.18287	2.54035
17	1.40024	1.52162	1.65285	1.94790	2.29202	2.69277
18	1.42825	1.55966	1.70243	2.02582	2.40662	2.85434
19	1.45681	1.59865	1.75351	2.10685	2.52695	3.02560
20	1.48595	1.63862	1.80611	2.19112	2.65330	3.20714
21	1.51567	1.67958	1.86029	2.27877	2.78596	3.39956
22	1.54598	1.72157	1.91610	2.36992	2.92526	3.60354
23	1.57690	1.76461	1.97359	2.46472	3.07152	3.81975
24	1.60844	1.80873	2.03279	2.56330	3.22510	4.04893
25	1.64061	1.85394	2.09378	2.66584	3.38635	4.29187
26	1.67342	1.90029	2.15659	2.77247	3.55567	4.54938
27	1.70689	1.94650	2.22129	2.88337	3.73346	4.82235
28	1.74102	1.99650	2.28793	2.99870	3.92013	5.11169
29	1.77584	2.04641	2.35657	3.11865	4.11614	5.41839
30	1.81136	2.09757	2.42726	3.24340	4.32194	5.74349
31	1.84759	2.15001	2.50008	3.37313	4.53804	6.08810
32	1.88454	2.20376	2.57508	3.50806	4.76494	6.45339
33	1.92223	2.25885	2.65234	3.64838	5.00319	6.84059
34	1.96068	2.31532	2.73191	3.79432	5.25335	7.25103
35	1.99989	2.37321	2.81386	3.94609	5.51602	7.68609
36	2.03989	2.43254	2.89828	4.10393	5.79182	8.14725
37	2.08069	2.49335	2.98523	4.26809	6.08141	8.63609
38	2.12230	2.55568	3.07478	4.43881	6.38548	9.15425
39	2.16474	2.61957	3.16703	4.61637	6.70475	9.70351
40	2.20804	2.68506	3.26204	4.80102	7.03999	10.28572

*Tables are reprinted with permission from Kieso and Weygandt, *Intermediate Accounting* (New York: John Wiley, 1983).

8%	9%	10%	11%	12%	15%	(n) Periods
1.08000	1.09000	1.10000	1.11000	1.12000	1.15000	1
1.16640	1.18810	1.21000	1.23210	1.25440	1.32250	2
1.25971	1.29503	1.33100	1.36763	1.40493	1.52088	3
1.36049	1.41158	1.46410	1.51807	1.57352	1.74901	4
1.46933	1.53862	1.61051	1.68506	1.76234	2.01136	5
1.58687	1.67710	1.77156	1.87041	1.97382	2.31306	6
1.71382	1.82804	1.94872	2.07616	2.21068	2.66002	7
1.85093	1.99256	2.14359	2.30454	2.47596	3.05902	8
1.99900	2.17189	2.35795	2.55803	2.77308	3.51788	9
2.15892	2.36736	2.59374	2.83942	3.10585	4.04556	10
2.33164	2.58043	2.85312	3.15176	3.47855	4.65239	11
2.51817	2.81267	3.13843	3.49845	3.89598	5.35025	12
2.71962	3.06581	3.45227	3.88328	4.36349	6.15279	13
2.93719	3.34173	3.79750	4.31044	4.88711	7.07571	14
3.17217	3.64248	4.17725	4.78459	5.47357	8.13706	15
3.42594	3.97031	4.59497	5.31089	6.13039	9.35762	16
3.70002	4.32763	5.05447	5.89509	6.86604	10.76126	17
3.99602	4.71712	5.55992	6.54355	7.68997	12.37545	18
4.31570	5.14166	6.11591	7.26334	8.61276	14.23177	19
4.66096	5.60441	6.72750	8.06231	9.64629	16.36654	20
5.03383	6.10881	7.40025	8.94917	10.80385	18.82152	21
5.43654	6.65860	8.14028	9.93357	12.10031	21.64475	22
5.87146	7.25787	8.95430	11.02627	13.55235	24.89146	23
6.34118	7.91108	9.84973	12.23916	15.17863	28.62518	24
6.84847	8.62308	10.83471	13.58546	17.00000	32.91895	25
7.39635	9.39916	11.91818	15.07986	19.04007	37.85680	26
7.98806	10.24508	13.10999	16.73865	21.32488	43.53532	27
8.62711	11.16714	14.42099	18.57990	23.88387	50.06561	28
9.31727	12.17218	15.86309	20.62369	26.74993	57.57545	29
10.06266	13.26768	17.44940	22.89230	29.95992	66.21177	30
10.86767	14.46177	19.19434	25.41045	33.55511	76.14354	31
11.73708	15.76333	21.11378	28.20560	37.58173	87.56507	32
12.67605	17.18203	23.22515	31.30821	42.09153	100.69983	33
13.69013	18.72841	25.54767	34.75212	47.14252	115.80480	34
14.78534	20.41397	28.10244	38.57485	52.79962	133.17552	35
15.96817	22.25123	30.91268	42.81808	59.13557	153.15185	36
17.24563	24.25384	34.00395	47.52807	66.23184	176.12463	37
18.62528	26.43668	37.40434	52.75616	74.17966	202.54332	38
20.11530	28.81598	41.14479	58.55934	83.08122	232.92482	39
21.72452	31.40942	45.25926	65.00087	93.05097	267.86355	40

Table 2   Future Value of Annuity of $1.00

$$A_{\overline{n}|i} = \frac{(1 + i)^n - 1}{i}$$

(n) Periods	2%	2½%	3%	4%	5%	6%
1	1.00000	1.00000	1.00000	1.00000	1.00000	1.00000
2	2.02000	2.02500	2.03000	2.04000	2.05000	2.06000
3	3.06040	3.07563	3.09090	3.12160	3.15250	3.18360
4	4.12161	4.15252	4.18363	4.24646	4.31013	4.37462
5	5.20404	5.25633	5.30914	5.41632	5.52563	5.63709
6	6.30812	6.38774	6.46841	6.63298	6.80191	6.97532
7	7.43428	7.54743	7.66246	7.89829	8.14201	8.39384
8	8.58297	8.73612	8.89234	9.21423	9.54911	9.89747
9	9.75463	9.95452	10.15911	10.58280	11.02656	11.49132
10	10.94972	11.20338	11.46338	12.00611	12.57789	13.18079
11	12.16872	12.48347	12.80780	13.48635	14.20679	14.97164
12	13.41209	13.79555	14.19203	15.02581	15.91713	16.86994
13	14.68033	15.14044	15.61779	16.62684	17.71298	18.88214
14	15.97394	16.51895	17.08632	18.29191	19.59863	21.01507
15	17.29342	17.93193	18.59891	20.02359	21.57856	23.27597
16	18.63929	19.38022	20.15688	21.82453	23.65749	25.67253
17	20.01207	20.86473	21.76159	23.69751	25.84037	28.21288
18	21.41231	22.38635	23.41444	25.64541	28.13238	30.90565
19	22.84056	23.94601	25.11687	27.67123	30.53900	33.75999
20	24.29737	25.54466	26.87037	29.77808	33.06595	36.78559
21	25.78332	27.18327	28.67649	31.96920	35.71925	39.99273
22	27.29898	28.86286	30.53678	34.24797	38.50521	43.39229
23	28.84496	30.58443	32.45288	36.61789	41.43048	46.99583
24	30.42186	32.34904	34.42647	39.08260	44.50200	50.81558
25	32.03030	34.15776	36.45926	41.64591	47.72710	54.86451
26	33.67091	36.01171	38.55304	44.31174	51.11345	59.15638
27	35.34432	37.91200	40.70963	47.08421	54.66913	63.70577
28	37.05121	39.85980	42.93092	49.96758	58.40258	68.52811
29	38.79223	41.85630	45.21885	52.96629	62.32271	73.63980
30	40.56808	43.90270	47.57542	56.08494	66.43885	79.05819
31	42.37944	46.00027	50.00268	59.32834	70.76079	84.80168
32	44.22703	48.15028	52.50276	62.70147	75.29883	90.88978
33	46.11157	50.35403	55.07784	66.20953	80.06377	97.34316
34	48.03380	52.61289	57.73018	69.85791	85.06696	104.18376
35	49.99448	54.92821	60.46208	73.65222	90.32031	111.43478
36	51.99437	57.30141	63.27594	77.59831	95.83632	119.12087
37	54.03425	59.73395	66.17422	81.70225	101.62814	127.26812
38	56.11494	62.22730	69.15945	85.97034	107.70955	135.90421
39	58.23724	64.78298	72.23423	90.40915	114.09502	145.05846
40	60.40198	67.40255	75.40126	95.02552	120.79977	154.76197

8%	9%	10%	11%	12%	15%	(n) Periods
1.00000	1.00000	1.00000	1.00000	1.00000	1.00000	1
2.08000	2.09000	2.10000	2.11000	2.12000	2.15000	2
3.24640	3.27810	3.31000	3.34210	3.37440	3.47250	3
4.50611	4.57313	4.64100	4.70973	4.77933	4.99338	4
5.86660	5.98471	6.10510	6.22780	6.35285	6.74238	5
7.33592	7.52334	7.71561	7.91286	8.11519	8.75374	6
8.92280	9.20044	9.48717	9.78327	10.08901	11.06680	7
10.63663	11.02847	11.43589	11.85943	12.29969	13.72682	8
12.48756	13.02104	13.57948	14.16397	14.77566	16.78584	9
14.48656	15.19293	15.93743	16.72201	17.54874	20.30372	10
16.64549	17.56029	18.53117	19.56143	20.65458	24.34928	11
18.97713	20.14072	21.38428	22.71319	24.13313	29.00167	12
21.49530	22.95339	24.52271	26.21164	28.02911	34.35192	13
24.21492	26.01919	27.97498	30.09492	32.39260	40.50471	14
27.15211	29.36092	31.77248	34.40536	37.27972	47.58041	15
30.32428	33.00340	35.94973	39.18995	42.75328	55.71747	16
33.75023	36.97371	40.54470	44.50084	48.88367	65.07509	17
37.45024	41.30134	45.59917	50.39593	55.74972	75.83636	18
41.44626	46.01846	51.15909	56.93949	63.43968	88.21181	19
45.76196	51.16012	57.27500	64.20283	72.05244	102.44358	20
50.42292	56.76453	64.00250	72.26514	81.69874	118.81012	21
55.45676	62.87334	71.40275	81.21431	92.50258	137.63164	22
60.89330	69.53194	79.54302	91.14788	104.60289	159.27638	23
66.76476	76.78981	88.49733	102.17415	118.15524	184.16784	24
73.10594	84.70090	98.34706	114.41331	133.33387	212.79302	25
79.95442	93.32398	109.18177	127.99877	150.33393	245.71197	26
87.35077	102.72314	121.09994	143.07864	169.37401	283.56877	27
95.33883	112.96822	134.20994	159.81729	190.69889	327.10408	28
103.96594	124.13536	148.63093	178.39719	214.58275	377.16969	29
113.28321	136.30754	164.49402	199.02088	241.33268	434.74515	30
123.34587	149.57522	181.94343	221.91317	271.29261	500.95692	31
134.21354	164.03699	201.13777	247.32362	304.84772	577.10046	32
145.95062	179.80032	222.25154	275.52922	342.42945	644.66553	33
158.62667	196.98234	245.47670	306.83744	384.52098	765.36535	34
172.31680	215.71076	271.02437	341.58955	431.66350	881.17016	35
187.10215	236.12472	299.12681	380.16441	484.46312	1014.34568	36
203.07032	258.37595	330.03949	422.98249	543.59869	1167.49753	37
220.31595	282.62978	364.04343	470.51056	609.83053	1343.62216	38
238.94122	309.06646	401.44778	523.26673	684.01020	1546.16549	39
259.05652	337.88245	442.59256	581.82607	767.09142	1779.09031	40

Table 3 Present Value of $1.00

$$p_{\overline{n}|i} = \frac{1}{(1 + i)^n} = (1 + i)^{-n}$$

(n) Periods	2%	2½%	3%	4%	5%	6%
1	.98039	.97561	.97087	.96154	.95238	.94340
2	.96117	.95181	.94260	.92456	.90703	.89000
3	.94232	.92860	.91514	.88900	.86384	.83962
4	.92385	.90595	.88849	.85480	.82270	.79209
5	.90573	.88385	.86261	.82193	.78353	.74726
6	.88797	.86230	.83748	.79031	.74622	.70496
7	.87056	.84127	.81309	.75992	.71068	.66506
8	.85349	.82075	.78941	.73069	.67684	.62741
9	.83676	.80073	.76642	.70259	.64461	.59190
10	.82035	.78120	.74409	.67556	.61391	.55839
11	.80426	.76214	.72242	.64958	.58468	.52679
12	.78849	.74356	.70138	.62460	.55684	.49697
13	.77303	.72542	.68095	.60057	.53032	.46884
14	.75788	.70773	.66112	.57748	.50507	.44230
15	.74301	.69047	.64186	.55526	.48102	.41727
16	.72845	.67362	.62317	.53391	.45811	.39365
17	.71416	.65720	.60502	.51337	.43630	.37136
18	.70016	.64117	.58739	.49363	.41552	.35034
19	.68643	.62553	.57029	.47464	.39573	.33051
20	.67297	.61027	.55368	.45639	.37689	.31180
21	.65978	.59539	.53755	.43883	.35894	.29416
22	.64684	.58086	.52189	.42196	.34185	.27751
23	.63416	.56670	.50669	.40573	.32557	.26180
24	.62172	.55288	.49193	.39012	.31007	.24698
25	.60953	.53939	.47761	.37512	.29530	.23300
26	.59758	.52623	.46369	.36069	.28124	.21981
27	.58586	.51340	.45019	.34682	.26785	.20737
28	.57437	.50088	.43708	.33348	.25509	.19563
29	.56311	.48866	.42435	.32065	.24295	.18456
30	.55207	.47674	.41199	.30832	.23138	.17411
31	.54125	.46511	.39999	.29646	.22036	.16425
32	.53063	.45377	.38834	.28506	.20987	.15496
33	.52023	.44270	.37703	.27409	.19987	.14619
34	.51003	.43191	.36604	.26355	.19035	.13791
35	.50003	.42137	.35538	.25342	.18129	.13011
36	.49022	.41109	.34503	.24367	.17266	.12274
37	.48061	.40107	.33498	.23430	.16444	.11579
38	.47119	.39128	.32523	.22529	.15661	.10924
39	.46195	.38174	.31575	.21662	.14915	.10306
40	.45289	.37243	.30656	.20829	.14205	.09722

8%	9%	10%	11%	12%	15%	(n) Periods
.92593	.91743	.90909	.90090	.89286	.86957	1
.85734	.84168	.82645	.81162	.79719	.75614	2
.79383	.77218	.75132	.73119	.71178	.65752	3
.73503	.70843	.68301	.65873	.63552	.57175	4
.68058	.64993	.62092	.59345	.56743	.49718	5
.63017	.59627	.56447	.53464	.50663	.43233	6
.58349	.54703	.51316	.48166	.45235	.37594	7
.54027	.50187	.46651	.43393	.40388	.32690	8
.50025	.46043	.42410	.39092	.36061	.28426	9
.46319	.42241	.38554	.35218	.32197	.24719	10
.42888	.38753	.35049	.31728	.28748	.21494	11
.39711	.35554	.31863	.28584	.25668	.18691	12
.36770	.32618	.28966	.25751	.22917	.16253	13
.34046	.29925	.26333	.23199	.20462	.14133	14
.31524	.27454	.23939	.20900	.18270	.12289	15
.29189	.25187	.21763	.18829	.16312	.10687	16
.27027	.23107	.19785	.16963	.14564	.09293	17
.25025	.21199	.17986	.15282	.13004	.08081	18
.23171	.19449	.16351	.13768	.11611	.07027	19
.21455	.17843	.14864	.12403	.10367	.06110	20
.19866	.16370	.13513	.11174	.09256	.05313	21
.18394	.15018	.12285	.10067	.08264	.04620	22
.17032	.13778	.11168	.09069	.07379	.04017	23
.15770	.12641	.10153	.08170	.06588	.03493	24
.14602	.11597	.09230	.07361	.05882	.03038	25
.13520	.10639	.08391	.06631	.05252	.02642	26
.12519	.09761	.07628	.05974	.04689	.02297	27
.11591	.08955	.06934	.05382	.04187	.01997	28
.10733	.08216	.06304	.04849	.03738	.01737	29
.09938	.07537	.05731	.04368	.03338	.01510	30
.09202	.06915	.05210	.03935	.02980	.01313	31
.08520	.06344	.04736	.03545	.02661	.01142	32
.07889	.05820	.04306	.03194	.02376	.00993	33
.07305	.05340	.03914	.02878	.02121	.00864	34
.06763	.04899	.03558	.02592	.01894	.00751	35
.06262	.04494	.03235	.02335	.01691	.00653	36
.05799	.04123	.02941	.02104	.01510	.00568	37
.05369	.03783	.02674	.01896	.01348	.00494	38
.04971	.03470	.02430	.01708	.01204	.00429	39
.04603	.03184	.02210	.01538	.01075	.00373	40

Table 4   Present Value of Annuity of $1.00

$$P_{\overline{n}|i} = \frac{1 - \dfrac{1}{(1 + i)^n}}{i} = \frac{1 - p_{\overline{n}|i}}{i}$$

(n) Periods	2%	2½%	3%	4%	5%	6%
1	.98039	.97561	.97087	.96154	.95238	.94340
2	1.94156	1.92742	1.91347	1.88609	1.85941	1.83339
3	2.88388	2.85602	2.82861	2.77509	2.72325	2.67301
4	3.80773	3.76197	3.71710	3.62990	3.54595	3.46511
5	4.71346	4.64583	4.57971	4.45182	4.32948	4.21236
6	5.60143	5.50813	5.41719	5.24214	5.07569	4.91732
7	6.47199	6.34939	6.23028	6.00205	5.78637	5.58238
8	7.32548	7.17014	7.01969	6.73274	6.46321	6.20979
9	8.16224	7.97087	7.78611	7.43533	7.10782	6.80169
10	8.98259	8.75206	8.53020	8.11090	7.72173	7.36009
11	9.78685	9.51421	9.25262	8.76048	8.30641	7.88687
12	10.57534	10.25776	9.95400	9.38507	8.86325	8.38384
13	11.34837	10.98319	10.63496	9.98565	9.39357	8.85268
14	12.10625	11.69091	11.29607	10.56312	9.89864	9.29498
15	12.84926	12.38138	11.93794	11.11839	10.37966	9.71225
16	13.57771	13.05500	12.56110	11.65230	10.83777	10.10590
17	14.29187	13.71220	13.16612	12.16567	11.27407	10.47726
18	14.99203	14.35336	13.75351	12.65930	11.68959	10.82760
19	15.67846	14.97889	14.32380	13.13394	12.08532	11.15812
20	16.35143	15.58916	14.87747	13.59033	12.46221	11.46992
21	17.01121	16.18455	15.41502	14.02916	12.82115	11.76408
22	17.65805	16.76541	15.93692	14.45112	13.16300	12.04158
23	18.29220	17.33211	16.44361	14.85684	13.48857	12.30338
24	18.91393	17.88499	16.93554	15.24696	13.79864	12.55036
25	19.52346	18.42438	17.41315	15.62208	14.09394	12.78336
26	20.12104	18.95061	17.87684	15.98277	14.37519	13.00317
27	20.70690	19.46401	18.32703	16.32959	14.64303	13.21053
28	21.28127	19.96489	18.76411	16.66306	14.89813	13.40616
29	21.84438	20.45355	19.18845	16.98371	15.14107	13.59072
30	22.39646	20.93029	19.60044	17.29203	15.37245	13.76483
31	22.93770	21.39541	20.00043	17.58849	15.59281	13.92909
32	23.46833	21.84918	20.38877	17.87355	15.80268	14.08404
33	23.98856	22.29188	20.76579	18.14765	16.00255	14.23023
34	24.49859	22.72379	21.13184	18.41120	16.19290	14.36814
35	24.99862	23.14516	21.48722	18.66461	16.37419	14.49825
36	25.48884	23.55625	21.83225	18.90828	16.54685	14.62099
37	25.96945	23.95732	22.16724	19.14258	16.71129	14.73678
38	26.44064	24.34860	22.49246	19.36786	16.86789	14.84602
39	26.90259	24.73034	22.80822	19.58448	17.01704	14.94907
40	27.35548	25.10278	23.11477	19.79277	17.15909	15.04630

8%	9%	10%	11%	12%	15%	(n) Periods
.92593	.91743	.90909	.90090	.89286	.86957	1
1.78326	1.75911	1.73554	1.71252	1.69005	1.62571	2
2.57710	2.53130	2.48685	2.44371	2.40183	2.28323	3
3.31213	3.23972	3.16986	3.10245	3.03735	2.85498	4
3.99271	3.88965	3.79079	3.69590	3.60478	3.35216	5
4.62288	4.48592	4.35526	4.23054	4.11141	3.78448	6
5.20637	5.03295	4.86842	4.71220	4.56376	4.16042	7
5.74664	5.53482	5.33493	5.14612	4.96764	4.48732	8
6.24689	5.99525	5.75902	5.53705	5.32825	4.77158	9
6.71008	6.41766	6.14457	5.88923	5.65022	5.01877	10
7.13896	6.80519	6.49506	6.20652	5.93770	5.23371	11
7.53608	7.16073	6.81369	6.49236	6.19437	5.42062	12
7.90378	7.48690	7.10336	6.74987	6.42355	5.58315	13
8.24424	7.78615	7.36669	6.98187	6.62817	5.72448	14
8.55948	8.06069	7.60608	7.19087	6.81086	5.84737	15
8.85137	8.31256	7.82371	7.37916	6.97399	5.95424	16
9.12164	8.54363	8.02155	7.54879	7.11963	6.04716	17
9.37189	8.75563	8.20141	7.70162	7.24967	6.12797	18
9.60360	8.95012	8.36492	7.83929	7.36578	6.19823	19
9.81815	9.12855	8.51356	7.96333	7.46944	6.25933	20
10.01680	9.29224	8.64869	8.07507	7.56200	6.31246	21
10.20074	9.44243	8.77154	8.17574	7.64465	6.35866	22
10.37106	9.58021	8.88322	8.26643	7.71843	6.39884	23
10.52876	9.70661	8.98474	8.34814	7.78432	6.43377	24
10.67478	9.82258	9.07704	8.42174	7.84314	6.46415	25
10.80998	9.92897	9.16095	8.48806	7.89566	6.49056	26
10.93516	10.02658	9.23722	8.54780	7.94255	6.51353	27
11.05108	10.11613	9.30657	8.60162	7.98442	6.53351	28
11.15841	10.19828	9.36961	8.65011	8.02181	6.55088	29
11.25778	10.27365	9.42691	8.69379	8.05518	6.56598	30
11.34980	10.34280	9.47901	8.73315	8.08499	6.57911	31
11.43500	10.40624	9.52638	8.76860	8.11159	6.59053	32
11.51389	10.46444	9.56943	8.80054	8.13535	6.60046	33
11.58693	10.51784	9.60858	8.82932	8.15656	6.60910	34
11.65457	10.56682	9.64416	8.85524	8.17550	6.61661	35
11.71719	10.61176	9.67651	8.87859	8.19241	6.62314	36
11.77518	10.65299	9.70592	8.89963	8.20751	6.62882	37
11.82887	10.69082	9.73265	8.91859	8.22099	6.63375	38
11.87858	10.72552	9.75697	8.93567	8.23303	6.63805	39
11.92461	10.75736	9.77905	8.95105	8.24378	6.64178	40

INDEX